THE ART OF

ROMANCE

Cooking®

Lighting the Fire
with Passion

Featuring:

The Art of Romantic Feeding for Two Where You
Will Experience a Breathtaking Evening Romancing
Your Relationship.

Web Site
www.romancecooking.com

Easy Step-by-Step Instructions

The Art of Romantic Feeding for Two

The Art of Table-Side Cooking

All Recipes Designed for Two

Tips for Creating a Romantic Mood

and Much More.

Lonnie T. Lynch

Cover Designed by Lonnie T. Lynch
Cover Photos
Corel Professional Photos: Texture II Abstract Red Cloth Photo
Photodisc: Rose Photo
Herma Photo Objects: Fork, Wine Bucket, Grand Piano and Candles
Photos

Romance Cooking® is a Registered Trademark in the
United States of America

Published in the United States by

Lonnie T. Lynch

9850 Sandalfoot Blvd.,
P.O. Box #226
Boca Raton, Florida 33428-6646

Library of Congress Cataloging in process.

ISBN 0-9629277-3-2

Acknowledgments

To my mother, Joyce D. Agee, I would like to give special thanks. Mom, you are special. You showed each of us kids how important a family is, whether by tucking us in at nighttime, or by providing special times for the family to be together. While growing up, watching your special grace and elegance has certainly helped inspire me to appreciate that special touch.

And to Patricia, a special thank you.

To Ginnijo Seim, a special gift of love and understanding that you supplied, on a day-to-day basis, that gave me the inspiration to finish this book. I hope I now can help others build the kind of relationship that we have both found in each other.

Special Recognition

Bob Barry, my good friend always, I could not have done these projects if not for your valuable help and guidance.

I would like to thank George Galluzi for sharing his famous saying, "Don't be a jack of all trades be a specialist in one."

Good luck and thanks to all of you!

Contents

Welcome to the Art of Romance Cooking

A tone that is both elegant and romantic can be created during dinnertime, turning any night into a magical evening that will give both partners an enhanced enjoyment of their relationship.

In this book, I'll talk about creatively using Romance Cooking® as a means to enhance your relationship. I'll give you the ideas and recipes you need to cook easy dishes that you will both enjoy together.

Whether newlyweds or married a long time you can now create elegant, romantic moods by using music, candles, and exceptional dinners. By being creative and experimenting, you will keep the desire alive!

In this book, we will discuss using dinnertime to dynamically enhance your relationship. By learning to spend quality time before, during, and after dinner, you will be able to develop even closer intimacy with your mate.

We will also discuss some simple ways to be more creative while serving dinner, wine, and/or providing entertainment. We will discuss the simple recipes you can use to reach that ultimate feeling of intimacy with your partner.

I consider myself an expert in the kitchen, and I know how important an intimate atmosphere can be. Quality time, enhanced by just the right atmosphere, is very important and should be given with love.

A Few Words from Lonnie

While cooking, learn to have fun and be creative in your presentation.

Most of all — enjoy yourself. Entertainment is the spice of life!

Visit Our Web Site at
www.RomanceCooking.com

www.romancecooking.com is informative, fun, creative, and loaded with links to teach all of us that cooking can be romantic and fun.

New recipes you need to cook nice, easy dishes that you will both enjoy together can be found here.

Spread the word: After reading and trying the recipes and ideas in *The Art of Romance Cooking,* call or e-mail your friends and family and help spread the word that cooking can be fun and romantic. The web site is loaded with information on how to order books or sign up for a romance cooking seminar.

We will also discuss some simple ways to be more creative while serving dinner, wine, and/or providing entertainment. We will discuss the simple recipes you can use to reach that ultimate feeling of intimacy with your partner.

www.romancecooking.com will be an ongoing project that is continually updated with new information and links to make this a truly unique romantic site for everyone to enjoy.

Relationship Recipe

The following recipe has five essential ingredients. By following this recipe, you will create a closer relationship for both you and your mate.

Recipe for a Successful Relationship

Time

Make time to arrange and adapt your schedule. Always make and take time to spend with that special person. Otherwise one day you will wake up alone, with plenty of time on your hands, and no one with whom to share it.

Communication

Make time to exchange ideas through writing, talking, or feelings. Any relationship without communication is not a relationship at all. So when you form the words *I love you*, show it, just don't say it!

Sincerity

Don't fake it — take genuine interest in your partner! Every relationship needs sincerity to thrive.

Fun

For play or amusement. Don't make your relationship a chore. Let it come naturally. Enjoy having fun at home, or try walking through a park and chasing each other. We each still have a little kid inside of us; let your inner child play!

Creativity

Set the right mood by creating the perfect candlelit dinner, or take that weekend getaway you've been talking about for so long. Experiment: Exchange love notes, or try something more adventurous — like taking a hot-air balloon ride.

Add above ingredients to a large mixing bowl and toss gently. Garnish with a smile and serve with love.

Nurturing Your Relationship will Keep the Flame Burning Bright

Making love is only half the fun! Remember to spend time touching, caressing, hugging, and holding. There is room for more tenderness in everybody's life.

Each of us needs the experience of sensual touch to enjoy a healthy, happy life. As children, the sensation of mom or dad hugging us made us feel wanted. As adults, we need that same fulfillment. The warm nurturing feeling of being hugged, kissed, and touched will bring chills down your spine that will make you feel wanted and appreciated. That is why making love late at night and then going to sleep is nice but does not greatly nurture a relationship. Try making love before or after dinner, then make more quiet, quality time by talking and hugging. Caressing expresses more of what you feel and will make you feel much more loved.

What makes people stay in love? The answer is intimacy. Some people spend more time daydreaming of that exciting relationship than cultivating the one they have. Love your partner for who he or she is and not for who you would like him/her to be. Everybody is born with the gift of the golden touch. The trick is knowing how and when to touch, how to move, and what to do to make another feel pleasure in every way. The physical and emotional involvements in any relationship are the foundation of true and lasting intimacy.

Trust

As in any relationship, trust is a basis for having true intimacy, whether emotionally, morally, sexually, or financially. Take the leap towards trusting and believing in one another.

Quality Time

Again, I need to stress the fact that without making time for your partner, you will never become intimate. So make time for more quality time!

Honesty

Trustworthiness, sincerity, and openness are words to live by. Without them you will have no possibility of a meaningful relationship. Be open with your partner in all your needs. And always treat people as you would like to be treated.

Using Dinner as Golden Quality Time

As in any relationship, the fire was kindled when you first met, the talking, hugging, and caressing. These feeling can't wait to see each other again! By using some simple recipes you will keep the flame lit.

Using Dinner as the Key to a Better Relationship at Home

Regarding quality time, home should be the place to put talk into action. Start with quality time before dinner and a shared beverage. Cook together, serve dinner together, and clean up together. Take action now!

Dinner — A Time to Talk

Use this time together to talk. Again, quality time is the goal. Don't talk about work or family… become a good listener and friend. Don't pick on each other or discuss problems that you may have. Use this time as good, quality talk time, as when you first met.

Enjoy the Dinner — No Interruptions!

Quality time should not be rushed. Learn to take your time. Slow down the dinner and enjoy the passion created with time spent together.

Tell friends and family not to call or visit during these special moments.

Turn off the ringer and let the answering machine take phone calls. If it was important, they'll call back.

Flames Recipe

You control your own world, so make the time.

2	fun loving people
2	with consistent honesty
2	radiating with sincerity
2	with whispers of passion
2	with sensual destiny

In a large mixing bowl, add ingredients listed and toss gently. Serve with candles and satin sheets.

A Never-Ending Romance with Passion

The honeymoon had passion, love, and intimacy. So use that same formula and learn to keep it alive. It was the little things that counted when you first met the cards, the phone calls, a day spent in total passion. Remember the phone calls to say, *Hi, I was thinking of you.* and the note on the mirror saying *I love you.* What was, should always be.

Anyone who thinks of love as a "deal" made on the basis of need has set themselves up for a big fall. Remember to give and show your appreciation as you did in the beginning. Every day should have you feeling as if you are still on a honeymoon. Remember the passion while gazing in each other's eyes. What a feeling! Without passion there can be no fulfillment.

Flowers

A gift of beauty, a treasure that will bring an easy smile to a face that says *I love you, too!* It doesn't have to be a bouquet or a dozen roses to be special. One rose sends a message that will be appreciated.

Cards

It's the thought that counts! Isn't it special when you get a nice card for your birthday? Well every day can be special. So drop a card to say *Hi,* or *I love you.*

Breakfast in Bed

Once a week, take turns serving each other breakfast in bed. It can be fun and easy. Get a bed serving tray and always have a flower to add freshness to the air. From a bagel with coffee and juice, to an omelette with juice, be creative and let your love flow!

Forever Recipe for Special Moments

Those special moments are every day.

1	blooming red rose
1	special card
1	colorful balloon

On silver tray place above ingredients and hand to someone special.

Setting the Mood

Setting the right mood is important...

Candles and low lights create ambiance.

Music will soothe the body and soul.

What you wear can enhance the setting.

Candles and Lighting

When setting the mood, a dim candlelit room can work wonders. In this section, we will talk about using lighting to set the mood. Always use candles or a dimly lit setting.

Music

Music will soothe the soul and help you forget problems of the day. Here are a few hints. When selecting music try to use a long–playing tape or CD. The music will flow endlessly. Try to make the mood last as long as possible, without a lot of interruptions. Light, contemporary music is my choice because it does not hinder conversation and is easy to listen to. Jazz is also recommended. The choice is yours but remember that your partner, lover, or friend should enjoy the selection also.

Suggestive Attire

This way of dressing will not only make you look appealing, but will build your confidence by letting you radiate a seductive look. It's the responsibility of each of you to dress nice and look appealing for one another.

If just getting home from work, or after dropping kids at the baby–sitter, take a few minutes to shower or bathe and get refreshed. Always have a nice cologne or perfume on hand – one that your partner likes.

When dressing, you will have a wide range of choices.

Women have teddies, nighties, tank tops, mini-skirts, nightgowns, or sexy dresses to experiment with.

Men can use sexy underwear with loose–fitting clothes to show their chests or wear a suit with no shirt or underwear. Lower your inhibitions, and you'll have more fun and shared intimacy.

Mood Setting Ingredients

Create a warm, soft and sensual mood which to enjoy each other in.

2	long burning candles
2	hours of soft music
2	fun loving people with suggestive attire on

Light a candle, play some nice soft music, snuggle up and gaze into each others eyes.

Listen to Your Partner

A very important ingredient of any relationship is the willingness to listen to what your partner is saying, not just expecting to hear what you want to hear.

 We must seek to communicate with each other, not only with words, but in those moments in which the words *I love you* are silently expressed.

The best partner anyone can have is the one who listens to you when you speak and sincerely cares about what you are saying. As in any relationship, do not become so self-involved that you do not listen to what is being said. Don't always talk about your problems. While researching this book, a lot of women complained about how self-serving men are and how they don't listen to the woman's wants or needs. This depletes intimacy in any relationship.

To keep up with the times, men must overcome this tendency and start listening to their partners.

So I must stress to men and women — learn to have quality time and listen to each other. Write down some things that were said, for later, in an effort to communicate more effectively and see what happens.

Five Easy Keys to Better Communication

1. Let your partner do his/her share of the talking.
2. Make your partner feel important.
3. Avoid arguments.
4. Show respect and always be open–minded to the other's opinions.
5. Listen to what your partner is really saying and make effort to be sincere.

Communication Hints and Tips

The most comforting sound to anyone is the sound of their own name. Good unions are made up of small sacrifices. Always make a sincere, conscious effort to lend your partner an ear.

The Name Game Recipe

So now you're at the table with nothing to talk, take one word and ask a question?

2   people talking – What does the word mean to you?

You have 2 minutes in which to talk about the word.
Word Name Game Ideas: Fun, sexy, beautiful, honesty, and love.

Key Relationship Ingredients

Here is six key ingredients that ever relationship should have and deserves.

Appreciation

Learn to overlook the flaws of personality and appreciate the good qualities that each of you possesses.

Responsibility

Taking responsibility for your actions and non-actions alike.

Understanding

Try to see the world through your mate's eyes. Be sensitive to his/her emotions and do not presume to know all the answers.

Respect

Hold one another in high esteem and have respect for rights of others. Remember this when dealing with your partner. Everybody has feelings and we all need to learn to respect those of others.

Caring

Respond to the needs of your mate. This validates that he or she is special.

Love

Love is not judgmental. It's the knowledge that *we may be different but there is something that makes us alike.*

Mirror Recipe Special Notes

A show and tell recipe.

1   large mirror
1   dry marker
1   someone special to read

Using mirror and dry marker, leave notes of special thoughts to someone special.

The Memory Lane of Passion

If the drive for passion and glitter in your relationship starts to wither, try to recall your most passionate memories. Recall the first golden days when you first met. What made you fall in love? Where were you when you first met? Recall the church where you were married, the hotel where you spent your honeymoon. There are always elegant and endless memory lanes to follow, just like walks in the park.

When renewing intimacy with your partner, the past should play an important part of your relationship. Try not to dwell on the bad moments. Only dwell on the good ones. Memories and emotions work in strange ways. Sometimes a song brings back memories of the past or makes you cry. At times you will have an experience that brings back memories of the past. Memory lane is simple; visit places that bring back the diamond in your memories. Play music that reminds you of your wedding or special moments in your relationship.

So when using memory lane, be creative and have fun. Learn to recall those elegant feelings that kindled sparks then, and you will appreciate what you have now even more.

Use your memories to recall the past experiences that brought pleasure to you and your mate.

Ideas For Memory Lane

1. Visit the place where you first met.
2. Act as you did when you first met.
3. At dinner, recite your marriage vows to each other again.
4. Talk about old memories with your mate.
5. Use your mind creatively.

Memory Lane Hints

Use the past to review the history of your relationship. Reflect upon time that has gone by.

Passionate Fantasies

Steaming passionate fantasies can enhance any relationship. So learn to experiment and have fun living out fantasies of your own.

Acting out reasonable fantasies can be fun, engaging to both partners, and should add an intriguing playfulness to the relationship. A nice fantasy to act out is what we, as kids, called *playing doctor*. Take turns and learn about each other's body while examining. You find that *playing doctor* as adults is a lot more fun than it was as kids.

Men and women tend to fantasize in different ways. The psychology of men and women affects their physical performance and satisfaction differently. Men and women have basic sexual tastes that come from within. Even if they are different, they can meet in the middle.

It's a fact that men's sexual fantasies are kindled by visual desires of all sorts. Some women like to be romanced verbally. Not all women shun football and read romance novels. The mixture of sexual fantasies in human personality is vast and varied. I marvel at how strikingly different people are and yet how they can overcome this by letting down their guard sometimes.

Fantasy need not be *deviant*. It can be elegant and seductive. By exploring and acting out fantasies, searing passion can be unbridled in a relationship.

Passionate Fantasies Hints

Start your fantasies by talking, then uncover the pearls hidden within. This will enhance your desire for intimacy as a couple. Your imagination is the source of all fantasy. By using your seductive prowess, you become more liberated with the exciting aspects of making love.

How far is too far is up to you. Dress up as famous people, then meet and have dinner. Read about the characters to see how they acted.

Hot and Spicy Ideas

Take Turns Striptease Dancing.
Put on a Sexy Fashion Show.
Whipped Cream Fantasy.
Buy a Book on Making Love and Read it.

Fantasy Experience

Here is a simple fantasy.

1	cup whipped cream
10	maraschino cherries with stems
¼	cup of honey

Decorate your partner with the ingredients shown above. The fun is inevitable!

Simple fantasies are easy to create and act out — try using whipped cream and cherries, or just two candles by your bed, for a start, as one of you does a slow striptease to music.

Love Coupon

This Coupon Entitles Holder to One Creative, Private, Sexy, Fashion Show. Erotic, Exotic and Fun.

Gift To: _____

Gift From: _____

• For Fun and Pleasure • Great Gift Idea •

Aphrodisiac Talk

Food that arouses or is held to arouse sexual desire. An aphrodisiac is anything that arouses or increases sexual desire. Are there really some kinds of foods that have the effect of arousing sexual desire? I don't know. But shapes of food and fantasies will play a large part, as well as the atmosphere, with the right lighting. Music can have as much effect as the nature of food.

Does sex and food go together? Man has always tried to find ways to stimulate his sexual vigor through the use of food and drinks. In ancient Rome, they took their food while reclining on couches in the triclinium. You need to look no farther for examples of sex in the dining room.

Myth or Fact Aphrodisiac

The search and belief in foods as an aphrodisiac will undoubtedly brew beliefs and lead searches down many paths to find the truth.

Oysters, eggs, onions, and clams have shapes that suggest female sexual organs.

Bananas, sausages, asparagus, and celery stalks have a resemblance to the male sex organ.

All are ingestible.

More Aphrodisiac Talk

In ancient cultures it was herbal potions and magical rites, in today's society it is potent drugs. In any relationship drugs are not the answer and should not be used if there could be dangerous physical and emotional consequences for your health.

One of my all time favorite movies is *9½ Weeks*, watch and you will see what food will do to arouse sexual desire.

Aphrodisiac Stimulants

Certain foods that have been regarded as Aphrodisiac Stimulants.

Foods: Oysters, lobster, caviar, crayfish, soft roe, and truffles.

Condiments: Pepper, pimento, cinnamon, nutmeg, cloves, saffron, vanilla, and ginger.

Ancient or Exotic: Shark's fins, musk, and ambergris are just a few.

No that does not mean that you have to serve oysters, caviar, use musk oil, and add nutmeg and cinnamon to all your recipes. But, by using aphrodisiac as a subject to talk about you will unleash some humor, and suggestive thoughts into romance cooking. After all, Romance Cooking® is all about having fun and creating a sensual mood in which to eat, drink, laugh, and play.

Sensual Emotions

Rouse
Arouse – Provoke
Wake – Wake Up
Rousing: Inspiring and Stimulating
Creating Passion – Creating Romance or the Flames will Die

Choosing the Right Beverage

Try to get in the custom of serving wine with dinner in place of other alcoholic beverages. It is important to remember that wine does not have to be expensive to taste good. When you find a nice wine, save the label or make a note so you can find it again.

Simple Guidelines

Suggestions for serving wine are guidelines only. The actual choice is up to you. Many people drink red or white wine only, no matter what the menu. When romance cooking it is a good idea to have red and white wine on hand, as well as a selection of both dry and sweet wines. Dry wine is served before dinner and with all courses except dessert, when a sweet wine is usually called for. Champagne is appropriate as a cocktail, with dessert, or on special occasions. Always have some nonalcoholic drinks and fruit juices or soda on hand for those who do not drink.

Honeymoon Minted Mimosa

1	bottle champagne
½	quart orange juice
½	bunch mint leaves

Using chilled champagne, mix with orange juice, garnish with fresh mint and serve.

Other Drinks

The serving of liquor is at your discretion. But when you plan to serve highballs or mixers, you will need tall glasses and a lot of ice. This is also true when serving soft drinks.

Hints and Tips

Serve white wine cold and red wine at room temperature. Let vintage selections breathe a while before serving.

Eating and drinking with your loved one is an enjoyable experience.

If after dinner coffee is in store *see page 72 to 74* for *The Art of Table–Side Cooking Flambe Coffees.*

Romance Raspberry Wine

2	wine glasses
1	bottle white wine
1	pint raspberries

Fill glasses with wine to ¾ full, add raspberries to wine.

Passion Peach Champagne

2	champagne glasses
1	bottle champagne
1	fresh peach — peeled

Fill glasses with champagne to ¾ full. Peel, seed and slice peach. Place in champagne.

Special Occasions

On special occasions, champagne is appropriate as a cocktail or with dessert.

Entertaining Romantically with Style

Like many culinary skills, table setting is a craft. You can combine the elements of china, glass, silver, and cloth together to paint a beautiful picture.

Setting an elegant table, using just the right color arrangement, will make you feel proud of your work. You can also create this effect using little paper plates and plastic dishes to make things a bit easier. Whatever you use, make the table look clean and neat to enhance the beauty of the table setting.

Table Coverings and Napkins

These two items should complement and enhance each other. A clean colorful table covering will help set the theme and create an inviting atmosphere for your guest.

Place Settings

Hopefully, you already have place settings on hand: dishes, silverware, glasses, and serving trays. If not, shop for items that reflect your taste.

Placing Napkins

Where to place the napkin? Some people place it on the plate or in the glass or on the table. Create your own style.

Centerpieces

Every table should have an arrangement in the center of the table. Many variety and specialty shops carry a wide range of items. The centerpiece you select can be as simple as flowers in a vase. The main thing is it should always complement, rather than detract from, your table setting theme. The arrangement needs to be simple yet elegant, so plan well in advance.

Smart Food Shopping

Hints and Tips

How much should you spend? When planning a meal, stay within your budget. If on a tight budget, forget the appetizers and salads and serve main entrée dishes only. Simple, inexpensive meals can be elegant if planned well. Plan your shopping list ahead of time and try to stick to it, buying just what you need for food and beverages. Remember, it's the quality of the time spent dining that counts, more than the meal itself. Be on the alert for specials on staples and other foods; a penny saved can be used for other items such as candles and enticing outfits. Shop smart and don't overspend!

All–Natural Products – No MSG – Use Health Food Markets

When purchasing food, pay attention to nutritional labels to get the healthiest product for you and your partner. A healthy person begins with the diet. So take time out to read labels and learn what really is in the food you eat.

Vegetables and Fruits

Vegetables and fruits should be bought in season. Hunt for ripe, healthy-looking produce. Look for color, texture, and ripeness in all produce to ensure proper nutrition. Shopping among all the bright colors of the produce section can be the highlight of your day. If it makes things easier or your selection is out of season, purchase frozen vegetables. Always wash vegetables and fruits thoroughly before eating.

Poultry

Serving poultry is a very economical way to entertain. Chicken is by far the most popular poultry item. Dishes created with poultry such as turkey, Cornish hen, duck, and goose are welcomed treats on any dinner table. When purchasing poultry, check for freshness and buy the cut that will meet your budget. Whole chicken is generally less expensive than buying separate chicken pieces. You can also purchase poultry cut in eighths, quarters, halves, and whole cuts. So shop for price and freshness. Always cook poultry within two days of purchase and buy from a reputable store. Wash poultry thoroughly before cooking.

Meats

Specialty cuts of meat are steaks, chops, and cutlets. They are easy to cook and are tender and delicious. The grading of meat is based on a uniform method of identifying those characteristics of meat that affect flavor and tenderness. This will set the value of the meat. The top grade is USDA Prime, sold mostly in fine restaurants and butcher shops, and hard to find in supermarkets. The next grade is USDA Choice, which is readily available in supermarkets. Then follows USDA Good. If meat does not have a label, it is most likely USDA Good. When buying meat, there are a lot of different cuts, talk to your local butcher and find the cuts that fit your needs. Also, don't forget ham, pork, lamb, and veal cuts. Again, buy the cut and meat that will fit your budget.

Seafood

Like meat, seafood comes in many different cuts and varieties. Always purchase the freshest available products to insure a healthy dish. Seafood should be almost free of odor, have firm flesh and should not be sticky or slimy. Frozen seafood is always available. Buy from a reputable dealer. Fish comes in two types: flat fish and roundfish. There is a wide variety of seafood available such as shrimp, crab, scallops, and shellfish. Talk to your fish monger for the product that will fit your needs.

Dry Goods

Buy only fully professionally wrapped packages and no dented cans. Read labels carefully to get the best product for your money. More expensive does not always mean better. When cooking don't be afraid to use pre-made soups, sauces, and other products to make your job easier. Vegetables and fruits should be bought in season. Hunt for ripe, healthy-looking produce. Look for color, texture, and ripeness in all produce to ensure proper nutrition. Shopping among all the bright colors of the produce section can be the highlight of your day. If it makes things easier or your selection is out of season, purchase frozen vegetables. Always wash vegetables and fruits thoroughly before eating.

Shopping Hints

Plan Your Shopping Ahead of Time
Look for Values
Stay Within Your Budget

Add Zest with Herbs and Spices

The wonderful flavors of fresh herbs can add flavor to your relationship as well as your cooking. Spices are a necessity in every kitchen.

Herbs

Herbs are used to enhance the flavor in your dishes and add color. The proper way to use herbs is in moderation. When in doubt, add just a pinch at a time. Add herbs to the dishes near the end of the cooking time so the flavor does not boil away. With a little imagination, you'll soon be creating your own exciting combinations.

Parsley and chives can be used in relatively large quantities without altering the flavor of the dish too much. They will add a nice color to the dish when used at the last minute in cooking.

Bay Leaves
Chives
Chervil
Cilantro
Coriander
Dill
Fennel
Lemon Thyme
Marjoram
Mint
Opal Basil
Oregano
Parsley
Rosemary
Savory
Sage
Sorrel
Sweet Basil
Tarragon
Thyme

Spices

The history of spices goes back about four thousand years to the Far East. They add zest and character to cooking with their flavor and aroma. As a house chef, you should always have on hand a wide selection of herbs and spices to enhance the flavor of your dishes.

Using Condiments and Seasonings

The sensible use of seasonings can complement food and enhance its flavor.

Seasonings include condiments, sauces, relishes, and flavorings. Imaginative use of these items can intensify and improve the flavor of food. When using condiments to flavor sauces and seafood, use moderate amounts at first so as not to overpower natural flavor. Specialty gourmet products on the market are also fun to experiment with when creating exotic dishes.

Hints and Tips

For flavoring, use ginger, leeks, onions, shallots, garlic, horseradish, mustards. Specialty nuts, seeds, grains, meals, flours, and other starches are used to add texture as well as flavor.

Specialty Oils

Specialty oils can subtly change the character of your dishes. Every kitchen should stock the finest oil and shortening available. For salads, use the first pressing of olive and nut oils. Cooking oils should have a high smoking point. Canola, coconut, corn, cottonseed, grapeseed, lard, olive, peanut, rapeseed, safflower, salad, sesame, soybean, sunflower, walnut, and vegetable are just a few specialty oils available.

Specialty Vinegars

Vinegars are used to impart sharp, pungent, and sweet flavors into foods. You can create your own unique specialty vinegars to have on hand for a full range of romantic occasions. Balsamic, champagne, malt, raspberry, rice, red wine, sherry, tarragon, and white are just a few of the varieties used to add flavor to food.

Specialty Brand Condiments

Tabasco®, Worcestershire and Dijon mustard are just a few of the specialty brands on the market that you can use to change the flavor of your food.

Food Presentation with a Gourmet Flair

Gourmet food presentation is the arrangement of garnishes such as lettuce, tomatoes, and cucumbers on the plate and topping with carrots and parsley for a colorful arrangement. When preparing and serving romantic meals always attempt to keep the words *gourmet dish* in mind.

Garnishes

Garnishes are an edible, decorative accompaniment to prepared dishes, appetizers, and desserts.

Garnishes can be placed around, under, or on top of food, depending on the dish. They can be as simple as sprigs of parsley or as intricate as carved vegetables. Simple ingredients such as lemons, onions, or radishes can add suggestive eye-appeal to almost any dish. Garnishes can also complement the flavor of the dish, as with paprika and chopped parsley. A confetti of fine diced raw vegetables is a favorite of mine, sprinkled on the food and rim of plate.

The presentation of gourmet food relies on many subtle factors, from garnish to table design.

Table Design

Is achieved by matching china, place settings, glassware, and folding napkins, with special centerpieces and candle holders (*see page 19* for place settings).

Visual Focal Point on the Plate

Arranging food with other items to enhance its look and color creates a visual focal point on the plate. This also applies to appetizers, salads, entrées, and desserts. With a little imagination, you can create some romantically suggestive presentations.

Tools and Equipment

A properly equipped kitchen for the romantic chef need not be complicated. But you should collect a minimum supply of tools and equipment, such as wire whisks, mixing bowls, baking pans, pots, pans, strainers, potato peelers, etc. This will allow you to concentrate on the more romantic elements of your gourmet cooking.

Use the proper tool for the job this makes cooking easy and efficient.

Here are some suggestions.

Spatula: While turning or removing foods from pan, oven, or grill, use a spatula so the food doesn't fall apart.

Knives: Use the proper knife for the job. Use a paring knife for cleaning food and a chefs knife for cutting vegetables and large pieces of meat.

Blender: Use a blender for mixing dressings and making sauces.

Tongs: Use tongs for turning food so that kabobs and grilled vegetables will not fall apart while cooking.

Cutting board: Clean your cutting board thoroughly after cutting or preparing each food product. Do not cut poultry, fish, or meat on the same cutting board as vegetables without cleaning thoroughly first between each task.

Tools Hints and Tips

Keep knife blades sharp during use and store them carefully. Clean after each task! Work in a comfortable area, using a large, stable cutting board, and clean as you work, which makes doing dishes much easier.

This will make time for more playful activities after the meal.

Less Food Prep – More Quality Time

Efficient ingredient preparation is the key to gourmet cooking. Unless both you and your partner enjoy sharing kitchen chores, the less time you spend doing food prep, the better. If your partner does enjoy helping you in the kitchen, the hints below will help you work as a team. Either way, these techniques will help you both enjoy more "quality time" together.

Pulling out the cutting board and knives and creatively chopping, dicing, peeling, and washing need not be overly time-consuming. But, to be good in the kitchen, you must master food preparation. Your local butcher or fishmonger can do some prep work at the store, but you'll still have to do some prep on own when you get home.

Trying some of the techniques I've mastered over the years will give you more time to concentrate on your love life.

Mincing Garlic: Peel garlic before placing on cutting board. Either mince into small pieces with a very sharp knife or crush with a sharp rap of your fist on the handle of a sturdy knife placed over clove.

Chopping Parsley: Wash parsley. Roll parsley tightly between hands and lay flat on cutting board. Using a sharp knife, cut into small pieces about halfway down. Continue chopping parsley until fine. Place in a clean kitchen towel and wring out under cold running water. Place in bowl for later use. Always save some parsley sprigs for garnish on plates.

Chopping Onions: Chop off ends of onion and cut in half first; this makes peeling easier. Lay halves flat and make parallel cuts about ¼-inch apart. Cut again at right angles and onion should fall apart in a diced cut. (By washing onions before you chop you will help eliminate the odor that will make you cry)

Washing Lettuce: All lettuce should be washed before using. Cut lettuce and place in sink or a bowl of ice cold water. Swish around, and dirt and sand will fall loose. For crispier lettuce, add ice cubes to water first. Remove lettuce and drain in colander.

More Food–Prep Shortcuts

Here are some more techniques for preparing food that you will need to know. The dicing, slicing, and julienne of vegetables is an art form that every one should master.

Cutting Vegetables: In many fine restaurants, preparing vegetables has almost been elevated to an art form. The way vegetables are cut is important as it will effect the cooking method used in the individual recipe – small pieces will cook much faster than large pieces.

Julienne Style-Strips: To julienne vegetables such as carrots and rutabagas, first cut into ¼-inch thick slices; then cut into ¼-inch strips. To julienne vegetables such as peppers and leeks, cut in half, lay out flat, and cut into thin strips. *See page 114.*

Cubing and Dicing: Cut vegetables in ½–inch strips, then cut again at right angles to form cubes. To dice, cut strips only an ⅛–inch thick, and then into smaller pieces.

Slicing carrots, celery, green onions: Clean these vegetables under running water. To save time, slice in bunches held firmly against cutting board.

Cutting Peppers: Using paring knife, make circular cut around stem and remove. Chop off top of pepper and remove seed pod in a bunch using twisting motion.

Kitchen string: Many food items are easier to prepare and handle when tied securely.

Gourmet Sauce Preparation

Before starting any recipe, study the Romantic Signature Recipes Dressings and Sauces section *on pages 190 to 206.*

As any great chef will tell you, the secret to romantic cooking is in the sauce!

The supermarket has a wide selections of sauces available such as brown sauce, chicken stock, and clam juice so shop wisely and read the labels. In the Dressings and Sauces section I will teach some simple and basic methods to be used in Romance Cooking recipes.

The Importance of Sauces, *see pages 192.*
Thickening Agents, *see pages 192*

Sunset Coulis Collection

Romance Cooking is about having fun and being creative and part of having fun is the culinary side. In this section you will learn how to paint plates with some simple and easy coulis. Romance cooking is about being an artist and painting a picture setting.

The Sunset Coulis Collection are simple sauces that have the colors red, green, purple, yellow and are easy to make.

Art Studio Coulis Painting Ideas, *see pages 204 to 206.*
Cilantro Pesto Coulis, *see pages 205.*
Hibiscus Coulis, *see pages 204.*
Mango Wasabi Coulis, *see pages 205.*
Sundried Tomato Coulis, *see pages 206.*

Cooking Methods

There are many methods available to cook food. Most fall into one of the three categories. 1. Dry Cooking Method 2. Moist Cooking Method 3. Combination of Dry and Moist Cooking Method.

Baking and Roasting

Dry Cooking Method: Baking is cooking food in the oven using dry heat. Moist Cooking Method: Roasting is cooking food in the oven using moist heat to seal in natural juices. Most roasting is done at 325° F. When baking or roasting, use an oven thermometer.

Poaching and Steaming

Moist Cooking Method: Poaching is cooking food in liquid, at or just below the boiling point. The amount of liquid being used should be enough to cover the food you are poaching. The actual boiling temperature depends on the liquid being heated. Steaming is cooking food placed on a rack or in a special steamer basket, over boiling or simmering water in a covered pan. Steaming will retain the foods' flavor, shape, and texture better than poaching.

Sautéing and Pan Frying

Dry and Moist Cooking Method: Sautéing is a method of cooking food quickly, in a small amount of oil, in a skillet or sauté pan over direct heat. When sautéing, heat the oil in the pan before placing food to be cooked.

Grilling

Dry Cooking Method: Cooking on a heavy metal grate set over coals or other heat source. Your grill should be allowed to become very hot. When grilling, always watch for fire flare-ups. Grill marks make food look more tasty.

Deep Frying

Moist Cooking Method: Deep frying is cooking food in hot fat, deep enough to completely cover the item being fried. Use oils designed for deep frying. The oil should be hot enough so it just soaks in. If oil is too hot, food will burn. Recommended deep frying temperature is 350° F. Don't guess, use an oil thermometer.

Nutrition Tips for a Healthy Relationship

Proper nutrition is important to everyone. All your meals should be well balanced, using each of the five major food groups – Meat, dairy products, fruits and vegetables, carbohydrates (starches), and fat. If you improve your eating habits, you will not only look and feel more attractive, but you will have much more energy to devote to the more romantic aspects of your relationship.

Today's typical food market is a virtual cornucopia of choices that can challenge your nutritional resolve. With so many dietary choices comes unprecedented responsibility.

Americans have recently been recognized as notorious over-eaters. The new nutrition revolution teaches us to eat properly. We now know that many of today's health problems can be traced to poor diet. High blood pressure, cardiovascular disease, obesity, unexplained nervousness, and chronic aches and pains have all been traced to poor nutrition.

Healthy Hints

When using these recipes, always make adjustments to meet your particular dietary needs.

Use low-fat substitutes when possible.
Use lighter oils.
Eat smaller meat portions and more vegetables and carbohydrates.

Nutritional Hints and Tips

Today's new nutritional labels have been greatly simplified and indicate appropriate serving sizes based on a 2,000-calorie-per-day diet, which is actually sensible. When planning meals, take this information into consideration. It really isn't that difficult.

If reading the entire nutritional panel is too much to ask, simply compare the number next to the words "Calories from Fat" to the number next to the word "Calories." As a rule of thumb, if the number of calories from fat is more than a fourth of the total number of calories, consider this a "high-fat" food item. Either avoid it entirely or use it sparingly.

Packaged Foods

Study preservative names and additives and learn to avoid certain ones and try to buy only the products that fit your dietary needs. It really is a jungle out there, but by preparing yourself with a little knowledge, you can persevere and supply both you and your partner with a well-balanced diet that is good for you both.

Fruits and Vegetables

No fruits or vegetables are bad for you. They are health champions. Eat more of them and you will feel better. Most are rich in vitamins and other nutrients. Spinach, carrots, broccoli, garlic, peppers, cauliflower, and many more are great sources of potassium, iron, and body-cleansing fiber. So eat your fruits and vegetables, live longer, and feel both sexier and healthier.

Meats

Meats are an essential source of protein. The meat portion of your budget will be a substantial amount when added up yearly. So, be well informed about cuts of meat. Get both your money's worth and your nutritional values worth. The cut of meat you select depends on the cooking method the recipe calls for. Some fat content is necessary to ensure tenderness. Remember that meat is very perishable.

Poultry

How does poultry stack up when meeting your dietary needs? Very well. All poultry is high in protein. A 2-ounce serving of chicken breast meat has about 7 grams of protein. Turkey breast is lower in fat than chicken breast. Duck and goose are high in fat. Avoid the skin and you will cut the amount of fat in half. Processed foods such as turkey roll and chicken franks should be avoided because they contain preservatives such as phosphates and nitrates.

Seafood

Most seafood has high-quality, easily digestible protein along with minimum saturated fat, cholesterol, and calories. Fish has a polyunsaturated form of fat rather than the saturated variety associated with red meat. Seafood is also a good source of the B vitamins, B-6 and B-12, niacin, and biotin respectively. It also contains the dietary minerals potassium and iron, which the body needs in large amounts. Seafood can be a healthy choice for your dietary needs. If you're up for a romantic evening, try oysters. I've been told they really can do the trick!

Nutrition Facts Sample Label

Serving Size 1 envelope (13g) (makes 6 fl oz. prepared)

Servings Per Container 4

Amount Per Serving
Calories 50 Calories from Fat 10 %Daily Value*

Total Fat 1g	2%
Saturated Fat 0g	0%
Cholesterol 10mg	4%
Sodium 540mg	23%
Total Carbohydrate 8g	3%
Protein 2g	
Iron	6%
Riboflavin	4%
Niacin Folic Acid	4%

Not a significant source of dietary fiber, sugars, vitamin A, vitamin C and calcium.

*Percent Daily Values are based on 2,000 calorie diet.

Your daily values may be higher or lower depending on your calorie needs.

Sample Label

Ingredients; Enriched Egg Noodles {Wheat Flour, Egg Yolk, Niacin, Iron, Thiamine Mononitrate (Vitamin B1), Riboflavin (Vitamin B2), Folic Acid), Maltodextrin, Salt, Cornstarch, Chicken*, Chicken Powder, Chicken Fat, Yeast Extract, Onion Powder, Carrots*, Flavors, Turmeric (for Color), Chicken Broth*, Paprika (for Color), Parsley*, Garlic Powder, Whey, Spices, Nonfat Milk*, Egg Yolk.

Quality–Time Dinner Menu Planner

The use of this menu planner will help you coordinate your special dinner plans with what you will need.

What to Buy

_____

Menu

_____

Appetizer _____

_____

Soup and Salad_____

_____

Sorbet _____

_____

Entree _____

_____

Dessert _____

_____

Romantic Feeding For Two

_____

_____

_____

Table Side Cooking

_____

_____

_____

_____

_____

Helpful Reminders

_____

What to Drink _____

_____

What to Wear _____

_____

_____

_____

_____

Creative Ideas

_____

Music _____

_____

Lighting _____

_____

Flowers _____

_____

Special Plans

_____

_____

Quality–Time Weekly Calendar

The use of this calendar will help in coordinating your quality time together. So make a copy and each week take the time to fill in and enjoy the special moments.

Mon.	Tues.	Wed.	Thur.
_____	_____	_____	_____
_____	_____	_____	_____
_____	_____	_____	_____

Fri.	Sat.	Sun.
_____	_____	_____
_____	_____	_____
_____	_____	_____

Watch the Sunrise

Breakfast in Bed

Lunch at Home

Go Dancing

Watch the Sunset

Have a Picnic

"Quality Time" Oath

I do solemnly swear to take time out of my busy life to create and spend quality time with the love of my life and my family.

Romantic Signature Recipes

The Art of Romantic
Feeding for Two

The Art of Romantic Feeding for Two

A Creative Idea for Fun

"The Art of Romantic Feeding for Two" involves creating a platter of food for two. Then use one fork and take turns feeding each other. Along with this a candlelit atmosphere, music, and passion will warm the soul and heart.

Romantic feeding is tried every day in restaurants. Just sit back and watch couples taste each other's meals then smile at each other. We will take romance feeding to a whole new level. After trying this section, you will feel as if you are still on a honeymoon.

The Art of Romantic Feeding for Two

Atmosphere

Atmosphere is a magic touch that needs to be created in order to truly enjoy "The Art of Romantic Feeding for Two." To create a romantic atmosphere light some candles, play some music, and turn off all the lights. Now you have created a romantic mood with passion and intimacy all wrapped up in one setting. *Your home is your own fairy tale castle and you have to write the script for the role you want to play.*

The Art of Romantic Feeding for Two

Romantic Feeding Thoughts

❦ My favorite recipe in *The Art of Romantic Feeding for Two* is The Exotic Fruit Platter and the Hickory Smoked Chicken Salad.

❦ **Catching the mess:** When serving your loved one, use your hand, napkin or small plate to catch the dribbling that might occur while feeding each other.

❦ Close yours eyes and take turns feeding each other. Try to guess what you are eating.

❦ Your loved one will love being fed and getting all the attention that he or she deserves.

❦ Sit up close and gaze into each others eyes. Remember a person's eyes will tell a hundred stories.

❦ Take your time and make the *The Art of Romantic Feeding for Two* last for hours if possible.

❦ Talk and get to know each other.

❦ The Art of Romantic Feeding for Two will add a fascinating aspect to cooking. It will help take Romance Cooking to a whole new level where intimacy becomes a part of the meal.

The Art of Romantic Feeding for Two

Silver Platter

The silver platter is the showpiece of the kitchen. Elegant and graceful in design, this one-of-a-kind kitchenware does not need to be hiding in the kitchen. You are ready for a lesson in *The Art of Romantic Feeding for Two* when you place an appetizer, salad, or entree for two on a silver platter.

The Art of Romantic Feeding for Two

Quick Hints and Tips

❦ The Art of Romantic Feeding for Two is all about seizing the moments and enjoying the atmosphere that is created.

❦ Turn romantic feeding into a weekly ritual

The Art of Romantic Feeding for Two

Creative Hints for Using Your Romantic Senses

Create a romantic atmosphere with the closeness and intimacy that we all dream of. Here are the keys to unlocking the secrets.

Romantic feeding for two will make you use all of your senses. It's about opening yourself to your entire range of senses. Take time and let every feeling seep inside your flesh. Let these feelings travel through your nerves, until your senses light up with a kind of intimacy that shows. A much closer level of intimacy will be deposited in your fond memory bank.

Using Your Romantic Senses

❦ **Sound:** Sit close enough to hear the sounds of food crunching in your mouths. The music will soothe the soul.

❦ **Taste:** While tasting, close your eyes and see if you know what it is that you just eaten. Play games with your taste buds.

❦ **Sight:** Sit up close and gaze into each other's eyes. The sight of being fed will truly create a memorable romantic meal.

❦ **Touch:** While sitting close reach out and touch a knee or hold hands. Feel the fork in your hand as you feed your soul mate.

❦ **Smell:** The aroma of food and the smell of romance in the air will send a tingle up your back.

The Art of Romantic Feeding for Two

Recipes for You

The following is a list of *The Art of Romantic Feeding for Two* recipes that you can choose from. All the recipes in the *The Art of Romance Cooking* Cookbook may be used for the *The Art of Romantic Feeding for Two*. Just serve on a silver platter family style and use the ideas from Romance Feeding Thoughts *on page 35.*

Appetizers:
Crazy Fruit Display with Exotic Yogurt Platter, *see page 37.*
Quick Fresh Fruit Platter with Exotic Dippings, *see page 38.*

Beluga Caviar, Condiments and Toast Point Platter, *see page 39.*
Salads
Passionate Tangerine and Wild Salad Platter with a Tangy Lemon Dressing, *see page 40.*
Vogue Antipasto Salad Platter, *see page 41.*
Entrée
Grilled Georgia Peaches and Chicken with Mesclun Salad Platter, *see page 42.*
Hickory-Smoked Grilled Chicken Salad Platter, *see page 43.*
Mediterranean Chicken Breast with Roasted Garlic and Tri–Peppers Platter, *see page 44.*
Roast Rack of Lamb with Mustard Glaze and Mint Sauce Platter, *see page 45.*
Lobster Dom Pérignon with Pearls of Vegetables Platter, *see page 46.*
Dessert
After Dinner Ritual Mood Setting Display, *see page 47.*
Gourmet Passionate Dessert Platter, *see page 48.*
Fondue–Style Pound Cake with Caribbean Fruit Platter, *see page 49.*
Tempering Chocolate, *see page 50.*
Rose Petals, Stuffed and Dribbled with White Chocolate, *see page 50.*
Romance Strawberries Dipped in Chocolate Platter, *see page 51*

The Art of Romantic Feeding for Two

Crazy Fruit Display with Exotic Yogurt Platter

Light the candles, play some non–stop music, and place the fruit platter next to you on the table. Sit up close and take turns feeding each other. *(Hint: Use your hand or small napkins to catch any dribbles that might occur while feeding each other.)*

¼	small cantaloupe
¼	small golden ripe pineapple
½	medium peach or pear, peeled and sliced thin
1	large kiwi, peeled and cubed
3	large strawberries, washed and stem removed
6	large fresh blackberries
2	small cups of exotic yogurt, for example, wild raspberry or key lime pie

Wash, peel, dice and slice the fruit into bite size pieces. Using a medium size silver tray, place the fruit in the middle of the platter. Next take the yogurt and pour on the sides of the fruit. Now get ready for a wonderful time.

Light the candles, play some music, and turn off the lights. Snuggle up and enjoy the fruit and the company.

Take turns closing your eyes and guessing what you are eating. It is a fun game to try.

Yield: 2 servings

The Art of Romantic Feeding for Two

Fruit Suggestions and Dancing Taste Buds

Taste buds are unique. You can try foods that are hot, spicy, cold, or warm, and your taste buds will dance to different beats.

Here are some fruits and vegetables that will make your taste buds dance.

Exotic Fruits: Apricots, bananas, blackberries, blueberries, grapefruit, kiwi, mangos, nectarines, papaya, peaches, pears, raspberries, watermelon, red ruby apples, Granny Smith apples, oranges, tangerines, plums, and grapes.

Exotic Vegetables: Heart of palms, artichokes, banana peppers, avocados, marinated mushrooms are just a few.

The Art of Romantic Feeding for Two

Quick Fresh Fruit Platter with Exotic Dippings

The quick fresh fruit platter is a way to save precious time. While driving home stop and buy mixed fresh cut fruit already to serve from the produce department. Use any dipping sauce you like or use the exotic yogurt recipe.

1	quart fresh cut mixed fruit
2	small cups of exotic yogurt, for example, wild raspberry or key lime pie

 Place the fruit in the middle of a medium size silver platter. Take the yogurt and pour on the sides of the fruit. Get ready for a wonderful time.

Now light the candles, play some romantic music, turn off the lights and snuggle up. Enjoy taking turns feeding each other the fruit.

Wow! A quick and easy way to enjoy the start of a memorable evening.

Yield: 2 servings

The Art of Romantic Feeding for Two

Beluga Caviar, Condiments and Toast Point Platter

A little caviar, a little champagne, soft music, and the lights down low will set a romantic atmosphere. Take turns feeding each other. Purchase premium imported caviar to insure the best quality. Caviar should be served well chilled, in tiny bowls which have been placed on a bed of crushed ice. Choose from the types listed below, based upon your taste:

Beluga: Large grained and very expensive.
Osetra: Small grained, lower in price.
❦ **Sevruga:** Smallest grained, a prized choice.
Red caviar: Made from salmon roe – not a true caviar, like sturgeon caviar; appetizing and modestly priced.

Basic Recipe

1	ounce caviar
2	hard-boiled eggs, shredded
4	slices white bread
1	medium head radicchio
¼	cup small capers, drained
¼	small red onion, diced
¼	cup sour cream
2	lemon crowns for garnish, *see page 159*
2	parsley sprigs for garnish

Chop the chilled hard–boiled eggs into small pieces.

Toast the bread, trim off the crust, and cut into points.

Cut off the bottom of the radicchio and remove leaves to form four cups. Fill radicchio cups with shredded eggs, capers, onion, and sour cream. Place radicchio cups on half of the platter.

To serve, place radicchio cups on a medium size silver serving tray. Place the caviar in a small bowl bedded with crushed ice in the middle of the silver tray. Surround the serving bowls with toast points. Garnish. Now light the candles, play some romantic music, turn off the lights and place the platter on a table. Snuggle up and enjoy taking turns feeding each other.

Yield: 2 servings

The Art of Romantic Feeding for Two

Passionate Tangerine and Wild Salad Platter with a Tangy Lemon Dressing

A gourmet salad that is a meal in itself. Marinated Artichoke Hearts with Roasted Red Peppers.

Tangy Lemon Dressing

1	lemon rind, grated
½	cup lemon juice
¼	cup corn oil
1	tablespoon sugar
1	pinch salt to taste

1	roasted red bell pepper, *see page 105*
6	artichoke hearts, canned
6	Calamati olives
⅛	pound feta cheese
2	medium tangerines, peeled and sliced
2	cups wild mixed greens, escarole, chicory, arugula, dandelion, watercress, or sorrel
1	large fresh basil leaf for garnish

Roast one red bell pepper, following directions *on page 105*. Peel roasted pepper and slice into eight strips.

Preparing Tangy Lemon Dressing: In a large mixing bowl, prepare lemon dressing by combining lemon rind, lemon juice, corn oil, sugar, and salt. Blend well. Add roasted red peppers and artichokes to dressing, refrigerate for 20 minutes.

Toss wild mixed greens in large mixing bowl with dressing. On a large silver platter place wild mixed salad greens on one side of the platter. Artistically place red peppers, artichokes, calamati olives, feta cheese, and tangerines. Garnish with basil sprigs. Now light the candles, play some romantic music, turn off the lights and place platter on table and snuggle up and enjoy taking turns feeding each other.

Yield: 2 servings

The Art of Romantic Feeding for Two

Vogue Antipasto Salad Platter

Whip up a tasteful gourmet platter with flavorful cheeses, robust meats, and colorful vegetables. That will tantalize your taste buds. Mix and match foods to suit your taste.

¼	cup white tuna, canned
1	medium canned red pimento, sliced
2	medium pickled beets
4	jumbo pimento-stuffed olives
2	large hard-boiled eggs, sliced
1	small can marinated mushrooms
2	medium artichoke hearts, canned
1	thin slice cooked smoked ham
2	thin slices smoked pastrami
1	thin slice liverwurst
1	thin slice pepper jack cheese
1	thin slice fresh mozzarella cheese
2	large leaf lettuce leaves, washed
1	order Fantasy French Dressing, *see page 195*
1	pinch salt and pepper to taste
1	sprig of herbs for garnish (thyme, oregano, or basil)

Drain tuna and mushrooms. Cut meats and cheeses in bite size pieces. Place the leaf lettuce on a large silver platter. Artistically arrange meats, cheeses, and vegetables on the large silver platter covered with leaf lettuce to create a vogue feeding platter for two. Drizzle with Fantasy French Dressing and sprinkle with salt and pepper to taste. Garnish with sprigs of fresh herbs such as thyme, oregano, or basil. Now light the candles, play some nice music, turn off the lights and place platter on table and snuggle up and enjoy taking turns feeding each other.

Hints: For added flavor and presentation serve a couple of different dressings for dipping in small serving bowls.

Gourmet Meat Suggestions: Hickory smoked ham, and smoked turkey.

Yield: 2 servings

The Art of Romantic Feeding for Two

Grilled Georgia Peaches and Chicken with Mesclun Salad Platter

If available see if can find some fresh Georgia peaches. I've been told that they are the best. Light yet tasty. Use a quality blend of baby mixed greens such as frissée, oak leaf and green leaf for flavor.

2	6-ounce chicken breasts, boned and skinned
1	tablespoon garlic, minced
1	pinch salt and white pepper to taste
¼	cup olive oil
1	large Georgia peach, peeled, halved, and cored
1	red onion, sliced ¼-inch thick
3	cups baby mixed salad greens, frissée, oak leaf and green leaf

Georgia Peach Dressing

⅓	cup olive oil
2	tablespoons Dijon mustard
¼	cup balsamic vinegar
1	pinch salt and white pepper to taste
1	large Georgia peach, peeled, halved, and cored

Place chicken breasts in a medium size mixing bowl. Season with 1 tablespoon garlic, salt and pepper. Add ¼ cup olive oil and marinate for 6 hours. Refrigerate until ready to cook. *Do not use oil from chicken breast to make dressing.*

Preparing Georgia Peach Dressing: Combine the ¼ cup of olive oil, Dijon mustard, balsamic vinegar and 1 peach in blender or food processor and mix thoroughly. Season to taste with salt and pepper. Set dressing aside.

Brush grill lightly with excess oil and heat to medium-high. Grill chicken about 4 minutes on each side or until just firm to the touch and no longer pink. Meanwhile, brush onion and peaches with dressing and grill about 2 minutes on each side, or just until fork tender. Brush peaches with dressing another minute on each side.

Take the baby mixed salad greens and place on one side of the platter. Spread them out a little. Slice the chicken breasts and place them on other side of the platter. Slice grilled peaches and place on top of chicken. Dribble dressing on top. You are now ready to indulge in a pleasurable ritual of feeding each other. Light the candles and snuggle up. Enjoy taking turns feeding each other.

Yield: 2 servings

The Art of Romantic Feeding for Two

Hickory-Smoked Grilled Chicken Salad Platter

A little barbecue at the beginning of the night will create a meal to remember forever. A covered outdoor barbecue grill is recommended when using hickory chips.

1	10-ounce chicken breast
4	ounces hickory chips
¼	cup butter or margarine, melted
¼	teaspoon paprika
1	pinch salt and white pepper
2	cups mixed salad greens
1	small vine ripe tomato, sliced
1	small cucumber, peeled, seeded, and chopped
6	large pitted black olives
¼	ounce fresh mozzarella cheese
1	order Key West Lime Dressing, *see page 195*

Place hickory chips in water. Cover. Let stand for 30 minutes and drain. Fire up the grill and get ready. Brush grill lightly with oil and adjust grate to about 3–inches from hot coals.

In a small bowl, combine butter, paprika, salt and white pepper. Brush both sides of the chicken with basting sauce. Grill chicken for about 2 minutes on both sides, basting frequently with butter mixture.

Place drained hickory chips on coals. Close vents on both top and bottom of grill halfway to spread heat and let smoke circulate. *Use heavy-duty aluminum foil to form a bowl-shaped cover if grill is not equipped with one.*

Cover chicken and smoke about 15 to 20 minutes on hot grill; do not baste. Slice chicken breasts into 5 to 6 slices each. On a large silver platter place mixed salad greens on one side of the platter. On the other side spread the sliced chicken breasts. Artistically place tomato slices, cucumber, black olives, and mozzarella cheese. Serve with Key West Lime Dressing on the side.

Snuggle up and enjoy taking turns feeding each other.

Yield: 2 servings

The Art of Romantic Feeding for Two

Mediterranean Chicken Breast with Roasted Garlic and Tri–Peppers Platter

Can you imagine sitting by the Mediterranean during sunset and eating a chicken breast smothered in fresh garlic, peppers, onions? The only thing better will be gazing into each other eyes.

2	6-ounce chicken breasts, boneless
¼	cup olive oil
1	medium garlic bulb, sliced
½	cup dry white wine
1	medium yellow sweet bell pepper, sliced thin
1	medium red sweet bell pepper, sliced thin
1	medium green sweet bell pepper, sliced thin
½	small red onion, sliced
2	large mushrooms, sliced thin
2	large lemons, squeezed for juice
2	sprigs fresh oregano, chopped
¼	cup fresh basil, chopped
1	pinch salt and white pepper to taste
1	order Saffron Rice, *see page 189*
1	lemon crown for garnish, *see page 159*
1	large basil leaf for garnish

In a medium size baking pan, place the chicken breasts and set aside.

Slice the bulbs of garlic into 5 to 6 slices each. Slice peppers, onions, and mushrooms. Place in a large mixing bowl. Add olive oil, white wine, lemon juice, oregano, basil, and season with salt and pepper to mixing bowl. Toss thoroughly to blend flavors.

Place the pepper mix on top of the chicken breasts. Pour juice from mixing bowl on top of chicken and vegetables. In a preheated 350° F oven, bake for 22 to 25 minutes or until chicken breasts are done. Slice chicken breasts into 5 to 6 slices each. On a large silver platter place hot Saffron Rice on one side of the platter. On the other side spread the sliced chicken breasts and top with the pepper mix. Make sure you dribble the juices on top. That is where the flavors are. Garnish with lemon crowns and basil leaves. Now light the candles, play some nice music, turn off the lights and place platter on table and snuggle up and enjoy taking turns feeding each other.

Yield: 2 servings

The Art of Romantic Feeding for Two

Roast Rack of Lamb with Mustard Glaze and Mint Sauce Platter

This classical entrée is very enjoyable. The rack of lamb is cut from the rib. The meat and fat has been trimmed away from both sides of the bone.

1	whole rack of lamb, 8 ribs–each with fat trimmed off
1	tablespoon Dijon mustard
¼	cup bread crumbs
½	tablespoon fresh rosemary, chopped

Mint Sauce

2	tablespoons granulated sugar
¼	cup red wine vinegar
½	cup mint jelly
1	tablespoon mint leaves, fresh and chopped
½	cup Brown Sauce, *see page 200*

Have the butcher clean and shim the rack of lamb. Place the bones in the bottom of a roasting pan. Place the roast, meat side up, on top of the bones. Brush with Dijon mustard. Pat on the bread crumbs and sprinkle with fresh rosemary.

Preheat oven to 375° F. Roast lamb to desired doneness, usually rare to medium. Total cooking time should be about 12 to 20 minutes. Remove the lamb from the roasting pan and keep warm.

Preparing Mint Sauce: Warm the roasting pan over moderate heat until the juices are caramelized and fat is clarified. Pour off the fat. Return to stove, add sugar, and heat until sugar is caramelized (do not allow to burn). Add red wine and mint jelly. Scrape pan and simmer 3 minutes. Add brown sauce and simmer 5 minutes. Strain and degrease mint sauce.

Cut the rack of lamb between the ribs into chops. Serve 4 chops per portion, with sauce on side. Garnish platter with your favorite starch and vegetables. You are now ready to indulge in the pleasurable ritual of feeding each other. So light the candles, play some nice music, turn off the lights and place platter on table and snuggle up and enjoy taking turns feeding each other

Yield: 2 servings

The Art of Romantic Feeding for Two

Lobster Dom Pérignon with Pearls of Vegetables Platter

This classic presentation will highlight your culinary skills.You take the lobster out of their shells and coat them with a francaise mix. Then you make a sauce with champagne and top it all with caviar.

1	medium carrot
½	medium zucchini
½	small yellow squash
1	Saffron Rice, *see page 189*
2	Parmesan Tomatoes with Asparagus Spears, *see page 183*

Francaise Mix

2	medium eggs
2	tablespoons Parmesan Cheese
1	tablespoon parsley, chopped

2	6-ounce African lobster tails
¼	cup olive oil
½	cup all-purpose flour
1	tablespoon shallots, minced
½	cup Dom Pérignon champagne
½	cup heavy whipping cream
4	cups lightly salted butter, room temperature
½	large lemon, squeezed for juice
3	drops Tabasco sauce
2	teaspoons caviar, *see page 39*
1	salt and white pepper to taste
2	lemon crowns for garnish, *see page 159*
2	parsley sprigs for garnish

Preparing Pearls of Vegetables: Wash zucchini, yellow squash and peel carrot. Using a small melon baller, prepare tiny pearls of vegetables from carrot, zucchini, and yellow squash. Scoop from the fleshy skin of the zucchini and squash, so these pearls will show mostly flesh, with a little green or yellow skin color. *(The inside of squash is too soft and has little color).* Cook pearls in a small pot of boiling water 2 to 3 minutes or until they are tender yet crunchy. Drain and set to the side. Prepare, Saffron Rice, *on page 189* and Parmesan Tomatoes with Asparagus Spears, *on page 183*, set to side and keep hot.

Preparing Francaise Mix: Crack eggs into a medium mixing bowl and whip. Add Parmesan cheese and parsley. Whisk thoroughly.

Preparing Lobster: Remove shells from meaty portion of tails (Leave bodies on while doing this). Lay lobsters flat, belly side up and using a sharp knife, butterfly from inside out. Fan out a little to each side.

Warm oil in a large sauté pan, over moderate heat. Hold lobster by tails and dredge bodies with flour on all sides (Do not coat tails.) Next dip lobster, except tail in Francaise mix and coat. Place lobster in sauté pan and cook 3 to 4 minutes on each side or until a light golden brown. Remove the lobster tails and place on paper towels. If lobsters are not yet cooked, place in oven at 250° F until done.

Place shallots in sauté pan and sauté for 30 seconds. Next add champagne, and reduce until liquid is almost gone. Add cream and reduce until sauce thickens. Remove from heat and using a wire whisk, whip in the butter. Add lemon juice, herbs, Tabasco, salt and white pepper.

Using a large size silver platter, artistically lay out the Lobster Dom Pérignon with Pearls of Vegetables Platter. Start with the Saffron Rice and Parmesan Tomatoes with Asparagus Spears. Next place cooked lobster tails on platter and pour the sauce over the top. Place caviar on top of Lobster Dom Pérignon. Take reheated pearls of vegetables and sprinkle around platter. Garnish with lemon crowns and parsley sprigs. You are now ready to indulge in the pleasurable ritual of eating lobster and fresh pearls of vegetables with the one you love.

Yield: 2 servings

The Art of Romantic Feeding for Two

After Dinner Ritual Mood Setting Display

You have to experience a mood setting display in order to fully understand and appreciate *"The Art of Romantic Feeding for Two."*

1	bottle chilled champagne (optional)
½	pint fresh raspberries
6	Romance Strawberries Dipped in Chocolate, *see page 51*
8	Rose Petals, Stuffed and Dribbled with White Chocolate, *see page 50*
1	cup non dairy whipped topping
8	maraschino cherries with stems
2	hours of light romantic dance music, nonstop
2	long burning candles

Before dinner prepare the recipes for Romance Strawberries Dipped in Chocolate and Rose Petals, Stuffed and Dribbled with White Chocolate and set to the side for later.

Using a very large size silver tray, place an ice bucket with champagne, glasses with raspberries inside, Romance Strawberries Dipped in Chocolate, Rose Petals, Stuffed and Dribbled with White Chocolate, small bowl of whipped cream and maraschino cherries.

Place on a table when ready to make a romantic display of champagne Romance Strawberries Dipped in Chocolate, Rose Petals, Stuffed and Dribbled with White Chocolate, whipped cream and maraschino cherries.

After dinner help each other with the dishes and clean up. Go in the living room, turn on the music, light the candles and turn off all lights. Open the champagne and fill glasses. While sipping on champagne take turns feeding each other, talking, dancing, and enjoying the experience. It is special when spent with the one you love.

Yield: Special moments

The Art of Romantic Feeding for Two

Gourmet Passionate Dessert Platter

Sometimes in life you have to let go and enjoy. In this recipe you will indulge yourself in the wonderful world of desserts. You will experience flavors that are warm, soft, cold, and tart. The flavors and textures will be unforgettable.

1	small size Napoleon
1	mini size eclair
1	slice cheesecake
1	medium size cream puff
½	cup raspberry sherbert
¼	cup warm chocolate sauce
½	cup fresh berries
¼	cup Romance Whipped Cream, *see page 217*

Take a trip to your favorite bakery and let some body else do the work. Purchase the ingredients listed above. Place sherbert, warm chocolate sauce, and romance whipped cream into three small bowls. Using a large size silver platter artistically design your dessert platter. Start by placing the filled bowls on the tray. Next surround with pastries, cakes, and berries. You are now ready to indulge in pleasurable ritual of feeding each other.

Yield: 2 servings

The Art of Romantic Feeding for Two

Fondue–Style Pound Cake with Caribbean Fruit Platter

Find the fondue set up that has been in your cabinet for years. Get ready to use. This is a very creative way to serve dessert with mix and match fruits and sauces. It is a special dessert presentation.

8	small golden sweet pineapple chunks
1	small kiwi, peeled
1	medium papaya, peeled and seeded
¼	pint blackberries
1	cup exotic fruit yogurt
1	small pound cake
1	cup Kahlúa Chocolate Sauce, *see page 217*
2	large 8-inch wooden skewers or fondue forks

Prepare Kahlúa Chocolate Sauce, *see page 217.*

Wash and dry fruits. Cut pound cake and fruit into bite size squares. On a large size silver platter place the fondue pot. Light and fill with Kahlúa Chocolate Sauce. Place around the pot of chocolate sauce the fresh cut fruit and pound cake. You are now ready to carry out to the dinner table.

Using fondue forks or bamboo skewers dip the fruit and cake into the yogurt and chocolate sauce. Indulge in the pleasurable ritual of feeding each other fondue style.

Yield: 2 servings

Double Boiler Cooking

Whenever it is desirable to apply very gentle heat without the pan being placed on direct heat.

A double boiler is used. It consists of two pans, which can be metal, glass or ceramic, one fits inside the other. The bottom pan contains water and the top pan sits over (not in) the water.

The Art of Romantic Feeding for Two

The Art of Tempering Chocolate

Chocolate is temperamental. It burns easily and should always be melted slowly in a double boiler for best results.

If using a block of chocolate coarsely chop the chocolate to be tempered. In addition, finely grate a few ounces of unmelted chocolate. Melt chopped chocolate in a dry bowl set over hot water; stir until smooth. *See page for 49* for Double Boiler. Do not allow chocolate to exceed 115° F *(Test with a instant-read thermometer)*. Next, remove bowl from hot water and set on a towel for stability. Gradually add one spoonful of grated chocolate at a time, stirring until melted.

Melting Chocolate with a Microwave

The secret to using a microwave is melt the chocolate at 50% medium and stir often. Start with 45 seconds and then 20 second intervals. Constantly stirring.

The Art of Romantic Feeding for Two

Rose Petals, Stuffed and Dribbled with White Chocolate

Believe it or not, gourmet rose petals are available for the purpose of cooking and are quite tasty. However, confirm that they are pesticide-free when buying or grow the roses yourself. They make a romantic garnish for salads, entrées, and desserts. Experiment with different fillings.

14	large rose petals, rinse gently
¼	cup natural cream cheese, at room temperature
4	ounces white chocolate

When purchasing rose petals, make sure they have nice large, clean petals. Wash rose petals gently and pat dry thoroughly. Prepare 14 rose petals by rolling individually around small pieces of cream cheese. Set stuffed petals about ¼–inch apart on a baking sheet.

Temper white chocolate according to instructions above.

Place tempered white chocolate in a parchment cone *(on page 215)* or small pastry bag with tiny tip. Place finger on tip to hold chocolate in until ready to dribble. Quickly (before chocolate cools down) dribble white chocolate over the top of all the petals by going back and forth, covering half of each petal top. Place in the refrigerator for up to 6 hours. Because rose petals are perishable, they are best eaten within hours after preparation.

Serve on plates covered with doilies, or serve with your other favorite dessert, which could be you. Now light the candles, play some nice music, turn off the lights and place platter on table and snuggle up and enjoy taking turns feeding each other..

Yield: 2 servings

The Art of Romantic Feeding for Two
Edible Flowers

Some plant blossoms are edible. They make colorful and romantic garnish. However, confirm that they are pesticide-free when buying or grow the flowers yourself.

Edible Flower Varieties:

Acacia and mimosa blossoms; almond blossoms; alyssum; apple, peach, and plum blossoms; borage; chrysanthemums; daisies; daylilies; dianthus; English primroses; geraniums; hollyhock; jasmine; lavender; lilacs; lily of the valley; nasturtiums; oranges and lemon blossoms; pansies; pot marigolds; roses; squash blossoms; and violets.

Nasturtium blossoms will have a peppery flavor that is great for salads.

Rose petals are full of romantic oil that may be infused in creams and syrups. To extract their perfume remove petals.

The Art of Romantic Feeding for Two
Romance Strawberries Dipped in Chocolate Platter

Huge red juicy strawberries dipped in white and dark chocolate with a sip of brandy or champagne, will make a perfect ending to a lovely evening.

10	large strawberries, with long stems
4	ounces white chocolate
4	ounces semisweet chocolate, coating

When purchasing strawberries for dipping, look for ones with the stem still on them, if possible. Wash strawberries and thoroughly pat dry. Temper white and dark chocolate in separate small double boilers according to instructions *on 49*. Keep colors separate.

Hold strawberries by their stems. Dip one at a time lowering tip of strawberry into chocolate to cover half of the fruit. Shake gently to remove excess chocolate and place on a baking sheet lined with aluminum foil or parchment paper. Alternate with white and dark chocolate until all the strawberries are covered. Set berries about ½–inch apart. Place in refrigerator for up to 12 hours. Because strawberries are perishable, they are best when eaten within hours of dipping.

Serve on a plate covered with doilies or with your favorite dessert which could be you. Now light the candles, play some nice music, turn off the lights and place platter on table and snuggle up and enjoy taking turns feeding each other..

Yield: 2 servings

The Art of Romantic Feeding for Two

Other Fruits for Dipping in Chocolate Ideas

When dipping fruits in chocolate, make sure that the fruits are dried completely. Any excess moisture will cause the chocolate to seize or become stiff.

Fruits for Dipping in Chocolate Ideas:

Bananas, apples, oranges, raspberries, blackberries, seedless grapes, kiwi, pineapple, and papaya.

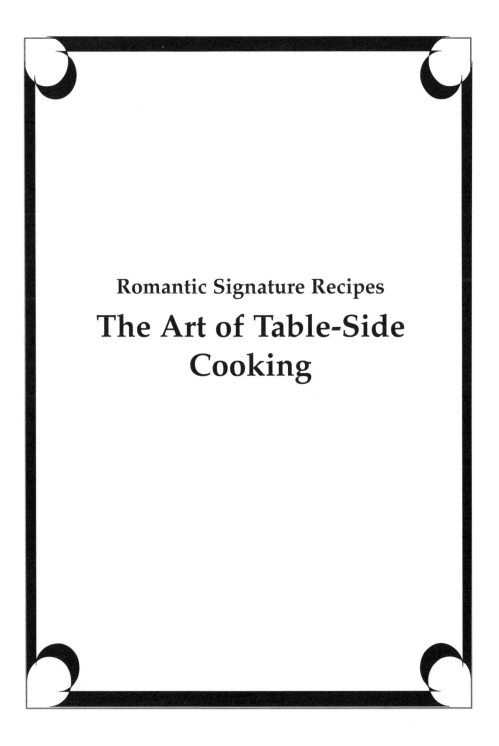

Romantic Signature Recipes

The Art of Table-Side Cooking

The Art of Table-Side Cooking

A Culinary Show Time

When cooking you are an artist that will dice, chop, and design a plate presentation. It is now time to learn culinary showmanship and have fun.

The Art of Table–Side Cooking is the art of putting on a mini show in front of a guest while cooking. Table-Side cooking is nothing more than preparing the food before your guest. It is simple yet complicated, if you don't know how.

Example: Light the burner. Place a 10-inch flambé pan on the burner and add 2 tablespoons butter. Then add ¼ cup of sugar and let the sugar melt. Add 4 tablespoons cherry juice, red currant jelly, and 12 black cherries to sauce, mix thoroughly. Turn the heat to high. Remove the pan at least 2 feet from the burner and add the liquor from a jigger. Replace the pan on the burner. Tilt the pan slightly and the liquor will automatically ignite. *(Safety tip – never pour liquor directly from the bottle near the stove.)*

Flambé means adding a high percentage of alcohol, such as brandy, rum, Grand Marnier, or whisky to pan, then igniting it for show and flavor. Serve directly from pan as soon as the flames die. This is an elegant and impressive way to serve dinner by putting on a show. Your guest will love watching and will learn and enjoy the creation that was displayed before his or her eyes.

The Art of Table–Side Cooking

The Heat Source (Burner)

The best known and most popular table burners used are butane and propane, They are regulated by a thumb-operated control. Tabletop butane burners provide an adjustable heat range similar to your gas stove. The heat source will be an important piece of the puzzle when table side cooking. The major characteristic of the stove should be size, control of heat, and stability.

Making a choice: Plain or fancy, a wide range of burners are available for every purpose. First decide on the kind of cooking at the table you're likely to do the most. Then choose the burner you find that will meet your needs.

Buy the best quality burner that meets the needs of safety as well as appearance.

Butane gas burners: Most resemble a top range cooking unit and are regulated by a dial or lever. They offer the highest heat and most efficient control. They come with their own black iron trivet.

Butane gas burners types: Iwatani

Mini electric stove tops: Assortment of mini electric burners are available in the stores. Find one that will regulate the temperature.

The Art of Table–Side Cooking

Fire Safety Tips

Safety Rules For Table–Side Service: A fully-charged Type ABC Fire extinguisher should always be near by. Or at least have a cellular phone at hand should you need to call the fire department. Never leave burner or stove unattended once lit. Stove and burner should be placed on a sturdy table that will not tip over. Keep flame at least 3 feet away from flammable objects such as drapes, hair, and clothing. Check for smoke detectors and automatic sprinklers. Make sure your fire insurance is up to date!

The Art of Table–Side Cooking

Flambé Pans

The heat source is important but now we will talk about flambé pans. Copper and stainless steel crepe pans are made for the purpose of taking a large amount of heat both outside and inside. They are deep enough not to overflow as the ingredients are rotated during finishing.

All copper crepe pans with stainless steel linings are ideal for housing flames in their interiors. But some of their shapes preclude flambéing large items such as steak, fish, or poultry. Steak, fish, and poultry main dishes will need deeper and more spacious pans.

So when purchasing copper and stainless steel crepe pans look for depth for recipes that will require a roomy pan.

The Art of Table–Side Cooking

Everything is Ready

One major key to the Art of Table–Side Cooking is having everything ready and then setting up the table for cooking.

To make your performance look smooth and skillful, place ingredients in the order in which they will be used for cooking. This will help keep things organized.

Every recipe will always entail a level of preparation that will be necessary.

1. Assemble your tools.
2. Assemble your ingredients.
3. Wash, trim, cut, prepare, and measure your raw ingredients.
4. Place all ingredients in bowls, pitchers, or on plates as necessary to set up table. Stove, plates, bowls, tools, etc.
5. Set up table with all equipment, ingredients, and utensils necessary to create the recipe.

The key to table side cooking is organization, which in turn will lead to greater efficiency.

The Art of Table–Side Cooking

Table-Side Setup Chart

A must study section if you are planning on doing table–side cooking.

Practice makes perfect, so set up and practice a recipe before putting on a public performance or at least do a dry run. Table–side setup is about laying foods out on a table in bowls and containers in an orderly fashion. If necessary place little marker notes like 1, 2, 3, and so on. Then perform a mini cooking show using the setup layout that will make your job look as easy as 123.

By preplanning and using the ideas from the table-set up chart your performance will look smooth and skillful.

1. Placing of Stove   2. Ingredients in Order

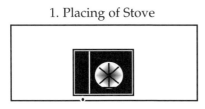 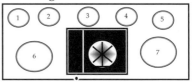

The Art of Table–Side Cooking

Equipment List

If you plan on doing a great deal of cooking in front of a guest, invest in some equipment.

The following is a list of equipment needed for Table–Side Cooking:

Gourmet portable stove and flambé pans.

Portable table on wheels, used for rolling equipment and ingredients to and from kitchen.

Assorted sizes of colorful bowls. Small bowls are used for ingredients. Large bowl for tossing salad.

A pepper mill, salt shaker, small pitchers for liquid, serving spoons and forks.

Fire extinguisher, long handle matches, table cloths, napkins, towels, chefs' apron and chefs' hat (optional but fun).

Art of Table-Side Cooking

Appetizer Shrimp Scampi Pernod

Next time you cook dinner, try table-side cooking. It is a lost art form of cooking that is fun, easy, and puts on a show. It's pure entertainment.

1½	ounces butter, cut into small pieces
1	tablespoon garlic, minced
12	medium shrimp, peeled and deviened
1	cup mushrooms, thinly sliced
2	ounces, Pernod liquor
1	ounce dry white wine
1	tomato, peeled and diced
⅓	teaspoon oregano
⅛	teaspoon rosemary
¼	cup heavy whipping cream
¼	teaspoon paprika
½	teaspoon Worcestershire sauce
¼	cup chives, chopped fine
1	ounce brandy
1	pinch salt and pepper to taste
2	lemon crowns for garnish, *see page 159*

Equipment Needed

1	fire extinguisher
1	portable gourmet stove and fuel, *see page 55*
2	long handled matches
1	large flambé pan, *see page 56*
11	small to medium size bowls
4	serving forks and spoons
1	jigger
1	black pepper mill
1	salt shaker
2	large dinner plates

Set up table for cooking using ideas from table–side chart *on page 57. Check Table–Side Fire Safety Tips before starting on page 55.*

Light the burner and set control to medium heat. Place a large sauté pan on the burner and add the butter. When butter melts, add minced garlic and sliced mushrooms. Cook for 3 minutes. Add shrimp to the sauté pan and cook, stirring for several minutes until shrimp is done. (Shrimp will turn pink when done.)

Remove the pan at least 2 feet from the burner and pour a 2-ounce jigger of Pernod into the pan. Place the pan on the burner and tilt slightly to ignite Pernod or use a long handled match. When the flames die down, add 2 ounces dry white wine and adjust heat to high. Add tomato concase, oregano, rosemary, paprika, worcestershire, chives, parsley, and brandy from a jigger. Stir to mix thoroughly. Add salt and pepper to taste. Cook for 3 more minutes, stirring constantly.

Arrange shrimp on two plates already garnished with lemon crowns and parsley sprigs.

Spoon the sauce over the shrimp and serve. Preset rice and vegetables on the table, family style, before cooking table–side. When done just sit and enjoy the meal.

Yield: 2 servings

The Art of Table–Side Cooking

Table-Side Hints and Tips

Showtime cooking can add a fascinating segment of fun to your life. Just ask people who know how to cook. They will tell you how they love the joyful anticipation of preparing each recipe. The art of table–side cooking will help those that love to cook take cooking to a whole new level where entertainment is part of the meal.

So here are some Hints and Tips for Cooking in Front of Guests:

Practice makes perfect so please practice a recipe before putting on a public performance or at least do a dry run.

Check the heat source for sufficient fuel to carry you through the cooking and serving. Always have extra fuel ready.

Always try to make your performance look smooth and skillful. Make it look like you know what you are doing.

Use long fireplace matches for the crucial moments of igniting liquor.

The Art of Table-Side Cooking

Pick Me Up Caesar Salad

This recipe gives directions for table–side serving, but can also be prepared in the kitchen.

Homemade Garlic Croutons

4	slices white bread
¼	cup olive oil
1	teaspoon garlic, minced
½	teaspoon dry basil

Pick Me Up Caesar Salad

1	large head romaine lettuce
2	teaspoons garlic, minced
4	anchovy fillets
1	tablespoon Dijon mustard
2	tablespoons red wine vinegar
1	large egg, in small bowl of hot water (or substitute 2 tablespoons mayonnaise)
½	cup olive oil
1	pepper mill
3	drops Worcestershire sauce
1	lemon, cut in half, in lemon wraps
½	cup grated Parmesan cheese

Equipment List

1	large wooden mixing bowl
1	medium mixing bowl for holding cut salad
2	wooden forks
7	small bowls to hold ingredients
1	oil and vinegar canisters
2	large chilled salad plates
1	small finger bowl, with warm water and lemon juice

Preparing Homemade Garlic Croutons: Take 4 slices of white bread and cut into bite size squares. Lay out on baking pan. In mixing bowl, blend olive oil, garlic, and basil. Dribble mixture on top of the croutons as needed while turning and tossing gently so they are evenly seasoned.

Bake croutons approximately 5 to 10 minutes or until dry and crispy with a light golden color in 350° F oven.

Salad Preparation — set up table for cooking using ideas from table–side chart *on page 57*, and lay out in bowls as shown.

In a large wooden salad bowl, combine garlic, 2 anchovies and mustard; mash into a paste using a serving fork. Add vinegar a little at a time, beating constantly with fork. Take egg from the bowl of hot water and separate the white from the yolk. Add the egg yolk to the dressing and beat until well combined. Dribble in olive oil while still beating mixture with the fork. Add a couple grinds of black pepper and the Worcestershire sauce. Squeeze the juice of ½ lemon through the lemon wrap into the dressing. Beat until smooth.

Add romaine lettuce and squeeze in the juice of the other half of lemon through the lemon wrap. Toss with salad forks. Add Parmesan cheese and croutons; toss until completely mixed. Wash your fingers in bowl of warm water and dry on clean cloth before serving. Arrange the salads on two large chilled salad plates. Garnish with 2 remaining anchovies and serve.

Yield: 2 servings

The Art of Table-Side Cooking

Passion Spinach Salad Flambé

A nice classic salad, that really puts on a flambé show while making.

Dressing

2	ounces corn oil
1	teaspoon red wine vinegar
3	drops Worcestershire sauce
½	medium lemon
4	medium strips smoked bacon, cooked and chopped

Spinach Salad

1	pound fresh spinach, torn into bite size pieces
2	large hard boiled eggs
1	pinch salt and pepper to taste

To Flame

1½	ounces brandy (100 proof)

Equipment Needed

1	fire extinguisher
1	portable gourmet stove and fuel, *see page 55*
3	long handled matches
1	large flambé pan, *see page 56*
1	small metal mixing bowl

1	wire whisk
1	small candle warmer (for dressing)
1	large wooden salad bowl
1	each wooden salad fork and spoon
1	small knife
1	jigger
1	medium ladle
2	napkins
1	pepper grinder
1	salt shaker
2	warmed salad plates

Set up table for cooking using ideas from table–side chart *on page 57. Check Table–Side Fire Safety Tips before starting on page 55.*

Dressing preparation: Light the burner and adjust the control to a moderate heat. In a small metal mixing bowl combine corn oil, red wine vinegar and Worcestershire sauce. Next squeeze the juice of ½ lemon through a clean white napkin, into the bowl. Add chopped bacon to dressing mix. Hold the bowl over the burner. Using a wire whisk whip until combined. Place the bowl over a candle warmer to keep the dressing warm until ready to serve.

Salad preparation: Place the spinach in a wooden salad bowl. Using the small knife slice the hard boiled eggs and add to the salad bowl. Add a few grinds of fresh pepper and a pinch of salt. Pour the warm dressing over the salad and toss with wooden salad fork and spoon until thoroughly mixed. Adjust the heat control to high. Place the ladle over the burner to warm up. Stand a few feet from the fire and pour in the brandy from the jigger. Place the ladle back over the burner. The brandy will automatically ignite. While still flaming, pour the brandy over the spinach salad, toss lightly. When flame is gone arrange on warmed salad plates and serve.

Yield: 2 servings

The Art of Table-Side Cooking

Fettuccine Alfredo with Prosciutto

This Fettuccine Alfredo recipe is for table–side serving. Do it once and it will become a routine in your culinary repertoire.

1	ounce whole butter, cut into small pieces
1	cup heavy whipping cream

1	large egg yolk
1½	cups grated Parmesan cheese
2	ounces prosciutto, thinly sliced
8	ounces fettuccine pasta, pre-cooked and cooled, *see page 102*
2	teaspoons parsley, finely chopped

Equipment Needed

1	fire extinguisher or cellular phone
1	portable burner stove, *see page 55*
1	large flambé pan, *see page 56*
2	large forks for tossing pasta
2	medium serving spoons
4	small bowls
1	medium bowl for pasta
2	warm serving plates

Check Table–Side Fire Safety Tips before starting on page 55. Next to the dining table, set up a small table with stove, equipment, and food for cooking using ideas from table–side chart *on page 57.*

Light the burner and adjust the control to moderate heat. Melt butter in sauté pan and add heavy cream. Bring cream to a simmer and lower heat, while stirring constantly. Add egg yolk. Mix thoroughly. Sprinkle 1 cup of Parmesan cheese, a little at a time, into the pan. Stir continuously until thick and smooth. Add prosciutto to the cream mix. Add cooked fettuccine and toss until pasta is well coated and hot. Arrange fettuccine on two plates, sprinkle with chopped parsley and a little Parmesan cheese. Serve with extra Parmesan cheese on the side.

Yield: 2 servings

The Art of Table–Side Cooking

Carving a Whole Roasted Chicken

A quick and easy table side carving station setup. Use tongs or a long-handled fork and sharp carving knife to serve chicken.

1	3-pound whole chicken
1	teaspoon salt
½	medium onion
2	large parsley sprigs
½	small lemon

2	tablespoons vegetable oil
½	tablespoon paprika
2	parsley sprigs for garnish

Equipment Needed

1	small cutting board
1	large tongs
1	long handled fork
1	sharp carving knife
2	large dinner plates

Place washed and dried poultry, breast side up, on a work surface. Season inside cavity with salt, add onion, a few parsley sprigs and half a lemon. Close cavity. Brush skin of the chicken lightly with vegetable oil and season with paprika. Truss chicken. (*see Trussing Poultry, page 118*)

Place breast side up on a rack in a large roasting pan. Roast in a preheated 325°F oven for 1½ to 2 hours depending on size, or until internal temperature reaches 180°F. Baste often. Remove to a carving board. Cover loosely and let stand 10 to 15 minutes. In the kitchen, remove the truss or skewers. Place chicken on a large platter and surround with parsley sprigs.

Now you are ready to carve: Use a cutting board and a pair of tongs or long-handled fork and a sharp carving knife. Hold the bird firmly in place with the tongs or fork and insert the knife between the thigh and the breast. Cut the skin and bend the thigh outward. Slice through the hip joint and remove the leg. Remove the second leg. Place the legs on a separate serving dish; slice the dark meat off the thighs and drumsticks. Slice diagonally down between breast and wing. Cut through joint and remove wing. Remove second wing. Insert tongs or fork into the side of the breast to be carved. Slice diagonally down from breastbone to the carving board. Lift off each slice and place on serving plates with dark meat and wings. Garnish with parsley sprigs and your favorite accompaniments. Serve.

Yield: 2 servings

Art of Table–Side Cooking

Flaming Samurai Swords with a Red Sea Sauce

With this recipe you will put on a flambé show. You will take cooked Samurai swords, secure in a pineapple half, dribble with 151 proof rum and ignite for a Flaming Samurai Sword show. When making beef kabobs always use a tender cut of meat. Two 15–inch gourmet metal skewers will work.

Red Wine-Soy Sauce Marinade

½	cup vegetable oil
¼	cup dry red wine
1	tablespoon garlic, minced
¼	cup soy sauce
¼	cup pineapple juice
¼	cup honey

Red Sea Sauce

1	cup tomato sauce
½	tablespoon chili powder
½	cup grated onion
½	teaspoon marjoram
½	teaspoon thyme
¼	cup dry red wine
2	tablespoons granulated sugar
1	tablespoon cornstarch

4	medium mushrooms, washed
1	red bell pepper, cut into squares
1	onion, cut into chunks
6	ounces beef loin tenderloin steak, cut into four 1–inch cubes
1	6-ounce lobster tail, cut into four 4 x 1 inch cubes
1	6-ounce boneless lamb loin rib chop, cut into four 4 x 1 inch cubes
2	cups Saffron Rice, *see page 189*
1	large pineapple with leaves attached
2	ounces 151 proof rum
2	long handled matches

Preparing Red Wine-Soy Sauce Marinade: Mix all ingredients listed for Red Wine-Soy Sauce Marinade in bowl and blend thoroughly.

Cut vegetables. Combine with beef, lobster, and lamb. Marinate in a large mixing bowl. Place in refrigerator for 4 to 6 hours.

Preparing Red Sea Sauce: Combine all ingredients listed for Red Sea Sauce and simmer gently for 15 minutes. Cool and refrigerate sauce until needed.

Drain meat mixture from marinade. Prepare two skewers alternating meat and seafood with vegetables. Grill or broil kabobs, turning and basting with Red Sea Sauce, 8 to 10 minutes or to desired doneness.

Cover two large platters with rice and Red Sea Sauce. Garnish with parsley sprigs. Place on dinner table.

Flaming Samurai Swords Presentation: *Check Table–Side Fire Safety Tips before starting on page 55.* Split pineapple in half lengthwise through the leaves. Place one half of pineapple, with leaves attached, flat side down on large silver serving tray with Flaming Samurai Swords laying on side of pineapple. Place a small cup with of rum next to samurai swords. Place silver tray on dining table. Pick up skewers and and insert securely into pineapple halves, at an angle. Balance and make sure that they will not tip over. (Remove any flammable items and make sure that skewers are not close to anything.) Dribble samurai swords with rum in a upward motion. Using long-handled matches, ignite and sit back in chairs and marvel at the flaming presentation. Serve kabobs on large platters after flames go out. Holding samurai swords from the top with a small napkins and fork, slowly slide meat and vegetables off of skewers one piece at a time. Place on top of a bed of rice already on plates.

Yield: 2 servings

Flaming Display Carry out to Table Setup:

Place one half of a large pineapple, with leaves attached, flat side down on a large silver serving tray. Place cooked skewers on the side of pineapple with a small cup with rum in it.

Flaming Display at Table Setup:

Pick up skewers with a napkin and insert securely into pineapple halves, at an angle. Balance and make sure that they will not tip over.

The Art of Table–Side Cooking

Lobster Love in Pastry Shells

There's lots a love in this Lobster Love Table-Side recipe!

1½	ounces butter, cut into small pieces
16	ounces lobster meat
1	ounce brandy
⅓	cup heavy whipping cream
⅓	cup tomato sauce
⅓	teaspoon curry powder
¼	teaspoon dried tarragon
1	pinch salt and pepper to taste
2	teaspoons parsley, chopped
2	Pastry Shells, *see page 131*
2	lemon crowns for garnish, *see page 159*
2	parsley sprigs for garnish

Equipment Needed

1	fire extinguisher
1	portable gourmet stove and fuel, *see page 55*
3	long handled matches
1	large flambé pan, *see page 56*
1	set of small bowls
2	each serving fork and spoons
1	jigger
1	pepper mill
1	salt shaker
2	dinner plates

Set up table for cooking using ideas from table–side chart *on page 57. Check Table Side Fire Safety Tips before starting on page 55.*

Light the burner and adjust the control to moderate heat. Place the pan on the burner and put in butter. When the butter melts, add lobster meat and cook, stirring for 1 minute. Remove the pan at least 2 feet from the burner and pour the brandy, from the jigger into the pan. Replace the pan on the burner. Using a long handled match light and place over the side of the flambe pan so the brandy will ignite. When the flames die down, push the lobster to one side of the flambé pan. Add heavy cream, tomato sauce, curry powder, dried tarragon and salt and pepper. Cook, stirring constantly; until the sauce becomes smooth and creamy. Gently combine the lobster with the sauce. Spoon the lobster meat and sauce into and over the pastry shells. Sprinkle with parsley. Garnish with lemon crowns and parsley sprigs, serve.

Yield: 2 servings

The Art of Table–Side Cooking

Steak Diane with Cognac Sauce

Club steaks are traditionally boneless, cut from the loin and often called New York Strip steaks. Use a good cut of meat so it will be tender. Pound meat out flat with a meat mallet to insure tenderness.

4	3 ounce club steaks, pounded out thin
2	ounces whole butter, cut into small pieces
1	ounce cognac
8	mushrooms, sliced thin
¼	cup green onions, chopped
1	teaspoon Dijon mustard

3	ounces dry red wine
½	large lemon, squeezed for juice
3	drops Worcestershire sauce
1	cup Brown Sauce, *see page 200*
¼	ounce cognac
1	pinch salt and white pepper to taste

Equipment Needed

1	fire extinguisher
1	portable gourmet stove and fuel, *see page 55*
2	long handled matches
1	large flambé pan, *see page 56*
1	set of small bowls
4	large wooden forks and spoons
1	jigger
1	black pepper mill
1	salt shaker
2	dinner plates

Set up table for cooking using ideas from table–side chart *on page 57. Check Table–Side Fire Safety Tips before starting on page 55.*

Light the burner and adjust the control to moderate heat. In a flambé pan melt butter. Season club steaks with salt and white pepper. Cook for 1 minute turning several times. Remove the pan at least 2 feet from the burner and pour a 1 ounce jigger of cognac into the pan. Place the pan on the burner. Using a long handled match light and place over the side of the flambe pan so the cognac will ignite. When the flames die down, move the steaks to one side of the pan. Add mushrooms, green onions, and mustard. Stir until mixed thoroughly. Slowly pour in red wine from jigger stirring constantly to combine. Squeeze in the juice of ½ lemon through a lemon wrap and add the Worcestershire sauce. Stir until mixed. Add brown sauce. Turn steaks and stir again until thoroughly combined. Add ¼ ounce cognac, into the pan. Add salt and white pepper to taste. Simmer a minute. Turn steaks several times, until completely coated with sauce. Arrange steaks on the plates. Spoon the sauce over the steaks and serve.

Yield: 2 servings

The Art of Table–Side Cooking

Romance Veal Marsala

The veal is pounded out into thin medallions and coated with Parmesan cheese for flavor.

12	veal scallops, pounded out thin
¼	cup Parmesan cheese, grated
1	ounce butter cut into small pieces
½	medium lemon, squeezed for juice
⅓	cup dry Marsala
1	teaspoon parsley, chopped

Equipment Needed

1	fire extinguisher
1	portable gourmet stove and fuel, *see page 55*
2	long handled matches
1	large flambé pan, *see page 56*
1	set of small bowls
5	serving forks and spoons
2	warm dinner plates

In th kitchen place veal medallions between two sheets of heavy plastic wrap and flatten to ¼–inch thickness. *(See Flattening Chicken Breast Tips, on page 118).*

Coat veal lightly with Parmesan cheese, remove veal and place on a plate.

Set up table for cooking using ideas from table–side chart *on page 57. Check Table–Side Fire Safety Tips before starting on page 55.*

Light the burner and adjust the control to moderate heat. Place the flambé pan on the burner and add butter. When butter melts, sauté veal medallions and brown lightly on both sides. Squeeze the lemon juice through a clean white napkin, over the veal. Add Marsala and cook for 1 minute, turning veal several times, mixing the sauce thoroughly. Arrange 4 veal medallions on each plate. Cover with sauce. Sprinkle with chopped parsley and serve.

Prearrange your favorite starch and vegetables on dinner table family style before putting on a show.

Yield: 2 servings

The Art of Table–Side Cooking

Bananas Foster Flambé

This is a romantic and impressive dessert served ice cream.

1	ounce unsalted butter, cut into small pieces
1	tablespoon granulated sugar
2	tablespoons brown sugar
2	medium bananas, peeled
1	ounce banana liqueur
1	teaspoon cinnamon
2	scoops vanilla ice cream

Equipment Needed

1	small fire extinguisher
1	portable gourmet stove and fuel, *see page 55*
1	large flambé pan, *see page 56*
1	set of small bowls
3	long handled matches
2	large serving spoons
1	small knife
1	jigger
2	napkins
2	desert plates with underliners

Set up table for cooking using ideas from table–side chart *on page 57. Check Table–Side Fire Safety Tips before starting on page 55.*

Light the burner and adjust the control to moderate heat. Place the flambé pan on the burner and add butter. When the butter melts add granulated sugar and brown sugar. Let the sugar melt, without stirring, and pour in banana liqueur, from a jigger, and adjust the control to high heat. Over flambe pan slice bananas into bite size pieces. Turn the bananas several times until heated but not soft. Add cinnamon. Remove the flambe pan at least 2 feet from the burner and pour white rum into the pan, replace the pan. Using a long handled match light and place over the side of the flambe pan so the rum will ignite. Blow out match and watch the flame.

When the flames die down, spoon bananas in a ring around each scoop of ice cream. Rotate the pan over the burner until the sauce boils. Pour the sauce from the pan over the ice cream and serve.

Yield: 2 servings

The Art of Table-Side Cooking

Cherries Jubilee Flambé

A dessert of cherries, spooned over ice cream. Either brandy or kirsch liquor can be used.

1	ounce unsalted butter
3	tablespoons granulated sugar
½	medium lemon
3	teaspoons red currant jelly
1	ounce kirsch
12	black bing cherries and juice
2	scoops vanilla ice cream, in stem ware or bowls

Equipment Needed

1	small fire extinguisher
1	portable gourmet stove and fuel, *see page 55*
1	large flambé pan, *see page 56*
1	set of small bowls
3	long handled matches
2	large serving spoons
1	jigger
2	napkins
2	dessert plates with underliners

Set up table for cooking using ideas from table–side chart *on page 57. Check Table–Side Fire Safety Tips before starting on page 55.*

Scoop the ice cream into two large red wine glasses and place in the freezer. Set the table up. Bring out the glasses of ice cream and put on a show.

Light the burner and adjust the control to moderate heat. Place a large flambé pan on the burner and add butter. When the butter melts, add sugar and let the sugar melt. Without stirring, squeeze the juice of ½ a lemon through a clean white napkin into the pan. Add 4 tablespoons cherry juice. When the juice is added the syrup will crystallize. With a serving spoon, stir until the sauce becomes smooth and thick. Add red currant jelly and mix thoroughly. Turn the heat to high. Add 12 black cherries into sauce. When the sauce begins to boil, remove the pan at least 2 feet from the burner and add kirsch, from the jigger. Replace the pan on the burner. Using a long handled match light and place over the side of the flambé pan so the kirsch will ignite. When the flames die down, spoon 6 cherries in a ring around each scoop of ice cream. Rotate the pan over the burner until the sauce boils. Pour the sauce from the pan over the ice cream and serve. Yield: 2 servings

The Art of Table-Side Cooking
Showtime Strawberries Sabayon

Sabayon is easy to make whether table–side or in the kitchen. Put on a show and enjoy.

3	large egg yolks
2	ounces Marsala
1¼	ounces Grand Marnier
3	teaspoons granulated sugar
2	cups sliced strawberries
1	cup Romance Whipped Cream, *see page 217*

Equipment Needed

1	small fire extinguisher
1	portable gourmet stove and fuel, *see page 55*
3	long handled matches
1	stainless steel mixing bowl
1	wire whip
2	serving spoons
1	jigger
2	napkins
2	dessert plates with underliners

Set up table for cooking using ideas from table–side chart *on page 57. Check Table Side Fire Safety Tips before starting on page 55.*

Light the burner and adjust the control to low moderate heat. In a stainless steel bowl, combine 3 egg yolks, Marsala, Grand Marnier, and sugar. Hold the bowl by the rim over burner with one hand and the wire whip in the other. Whip without stopping until mixture becomes thick and fluffy 3 to 4 minutes. Remove the bowl from the heat, spoon the mixture over top of the strawberries laid out on the dessert plate. Spoon whipped cream on top of the sabayon. Place dessert plate on underlines and serve.

Yield: 2 servings

The Art of Table-Side Cooking
Passion Coffee With Cognac

A wonderful after dinner coffee that is full of flavor and body. Practice makes perfect

1½	ounces cognac
1	teaspoon granulated sugar
1	small cinnamon stick
4	medium cloves
1	medium lemon
1	medium orange
1	ounce curacao liquor
1	small bowl of granulated sugar
2	cups of hot coffee

Equipment Needed

1	small fire extinguisher
1	portable gourmet stove and fuel, *see page 55*
3	long handled matches
1	silver bowl and platter
1	silver ladle
1	small sharp paring knife
1	each serving fork and spoon
1	jigger
2	napkins
2	demitasse cups and saucers
2	demitasse spoons

Set up table for cooking using ideas from table–side chart *on page 57. Check Table–Side Fire Safety Tips before starting on page 55.*

Light the burner and adjust the control to moderate heat. Pour the jigger of cognac into a silver bowl and add 1 teaspoon sugar. Next add cinnamon and 4 cloves. With a small sharp paring knife, peel lemon by starting at the top and peel in a circle around the fruit in thin spiral, being careful not to break the peel *(Practice beforehand on some extra lemons so when it's show time you know how to do it)*. Repeat the same procedure with the orange. Now with two long-handled serving forks, hold one end of the fruit spirals and dip in the bowl of curacao. Hold the fruit peel spirals over the silver bowl and sprinkle sugar over them. Hold a lit long handled match under the spirals and they will automatically ignite the contents in the silver bowl. When the flames die down, drop the fruit peels into the bowl and add 1 cup of strong black coffee. Mix thoroughly. Pour the remainder of the curacao into a large ladle and place over the burner. It will automatically ignite so hold ladle at the top of the handle. Pour the curacao into the bowl and mix well. Ladle the Passion Coffee into demitasse cups and serve.

Yield: 2 servings

The Art of Table-Side Cooking

Romance Coffee With Tia Maria

The fun of cooking is putting on a show and being watched. A stage is your dining room and your audience is your guest. Practice makes perfect so please practice before putting a show on in front of some one.

¼	medium lemon
1	cup granulated sugar in bowl
1½	ounces cognac
1½	ounce tia maria
3	cups of hot coffee
1	cup Romance Whipped Cream, *see page 217*

Equipment Needed

1	small fire extinguisher
1	portable gourmet stove and fuel, *see page 55*
3	long handled matches
2	heat resistant glasses with stem
1	serving spoon
1	jigger
2	napkins
2	desert plate with underliner

Set up table for cooking using ideas from table–side chart *on page 57. Check Table–Side Fire Safety Tips before starting on page 55.*

Light the burner and adjust the control to moderate heat. Rub the rim of a glass with lemon. Dip the rim in the bowl of granulated sugar to coat. Pour 1½ ounces cognac from a jigger into the glass hold the glass by the stem over the burner. Turning continuously to prevent breaking, until the cognac ignites. Remove the glass from the burner and swirl until the sugar on the rim caramelizes. Pour in ¾ ounces of tia maria. Add hot coffee to within inch of the top of glass. Add ½ teaspoon of sugar to coffee. Next, spoon romance whipped cream over top of coffee. For presenting, wrap the glass in a clean white napkin, place on a dessert plate with underliner and serve.

Yield: 2 servings

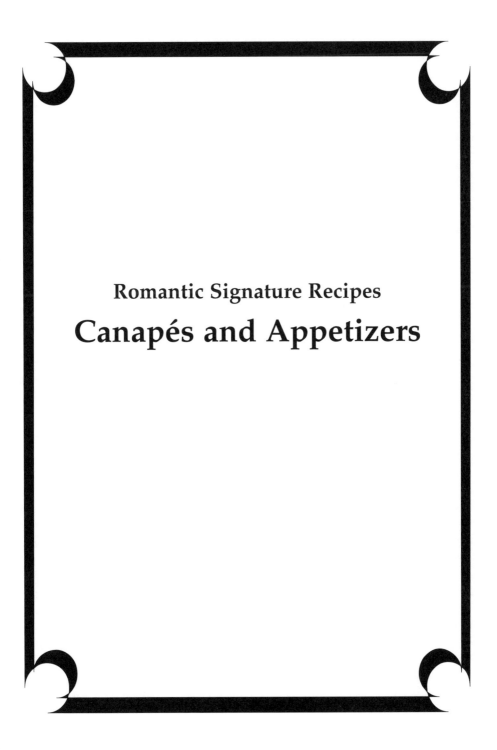

Romantic Signature Recipes

Canapés and Appetizers

The Commencement of a Relationship

Remember and enjoy the precious moments of a relationship when together each day. This is the commencement of things to happen. Set in motion the thrill of talking and caring about each other's dreams that you shared with each other.

Romantic Appetizers

Bubble bath before evening starts.
Special phone call that day to remind.
Exchange cards, flowers, and hug.

The Color of Roses All Have Special Meanings

Red Rose = Passion
Pink Rose = Friendship
Yellow Rose = Respect
White Rose = Purity

Classical Canapés as a Prelude to a Romantic Evening

Canapés are small, decorative appetizers that can be simple or elaborate. The following are a few simple ideas for creating canapés that you will find easy to make – and they taste great!

Cantaloupe with Prosciutto

Peel ¼ of cantaloupe and remove seeds. Cut cantaloupe in thin 2–inch slices. Wrap each slice of melon using thin-sliced prosciutto.

Celery Sticks with Boursin Cheese

Clean and wash celery, cut in 2–inch sections. Nick each piece of celery on round side so they will not roll over. Fill hollow side of each celery stick with boursin cheese by using a pastry bag or small spoon. Garnish with walnut and small parsley sprig.

Sour Cream and Caviar

Using two slices of toasted bread, cut into six small toast rounds by using circle cutters or top of small shot glass. Place a moderate amount of sour cream on top of toast rounds and garnish with caviar and chopped red onion.

Salami and Olive Swirls

For each swirl, roll one thin slice of salami around a large green or black stuffed olive in a cone shape. Secure with toothpicks. For easy rolling, cut each salami slice halfway through.

Shrimp and Pomery Mustard on Toast Rounds

Using two slices of toasted bread, cut into six small toast rounds by using circle cutters or top of small shot glass. Spread small portions of Pomery mustard on toasted rounds. Place 2 to 3 small chunks of baby shrimp on top of each piece. Garnish with fresh parsley sprigs.

Smoked Salmon Triangles with Dill

Using two slices of toasted bread, cut into eight triangular shapes. Place small portion of soft cream cheese on each triangle. Top with thin slices of smoked salmon. Garnish with a small piece fresh dill

Classical Canapé Display

When entertaining you will find it convenient to prepare canapé platters well in advance. With a little imagination, you can use canapés to set the mood for a sensual feast!

2	each Classical Canapé Selection
1	silver serving tray
1	medium paper doilies

Cover serving tray with doilies. Lay out canapés in a neat fashion and serve.

Plan on one dozen or more canapés but leave room to enjoy the main course.

Yield: 2 servings

Avocado Cocktail with Imperial Sauce

Let avocados sit at room temperature until ripe. You may add fresh shredded horseradish to the sauce recipe for extra zest

Avocado Preparation

2	medium ripe avocados
2	cups shredded lettuce
2	lemon wheels for garnish
2	parsley sprigs for garnish

Imperial Sauce

2	tablespoons mayonnaise
2	tablespoons catsup
1	tablespoon pickle relish
⅛	teaspoon Worcestershire sauce
½	tablespoon lemon juice
1	dash of Tabasco® sauce
1	pinch salt and white pepper to taste

Cut avocados lengthwise in half; remove pit; peel and cut into cubes. Place shredded lettuce followed by avocado cubes into two margarita glasses.

Preparing Imperial Sauce: Combine ingredients in small bowl, mix well. Spoon evenly over avocados; refrigerate at least ½ hour or until well chilled. Garnish with lemon wheels and parsley sprigs.

Yield: 2 servings

Sensual Crudités Display with an Erotic Creamy Onion Dip

A healthy appetizer. Arrange vegetables on plate covered with bed of leaf lettuce. Vegetables can vary depending on season and your taste buds.

¼	small head leaf lettuce
1	small red pepper
½	medium carrot, peeled and washed
1	medium celery stem, washed
¼	small head broccoli, florets only
½	small zucchini
½	medium yellow squash
8	large black olives, pitted

Erotic Creamy Onion Dip

¼	cup sour cream
1	teaspoon onion soup mix

Cover large plate with leaf lettuce. Cut one red pepper in half, remove seeds; place one half of red pepper in middle of plate and fill with dip. Next, cut carrots, celery, zucchini, yellow squash and remaining red pepper half into medium size sticks 2 to 3 inches long. Remove heads from broccoli stems. Arrange all vegetables on plate around red pepper bowl filled with dip. Serve immediately or seal with clear plastic wrap and place in refrigerator for serving later.

Preparing Erotic Creamy Onion Dip: In small bowl, combine sour cream and onion soup mix. Blend completely and adjust to taste. Mixture will thicken and flavor will be enhanced if refrigerated for one hour prior to serving.

Alternate Vegetable Ideas

Try using fresh asparagus, cauliflower, cherry tomatoes, cucumbers, yellow bell peppers, mushrooms or snow pea pods.

Yield: 2 servings

Tempting Cheese Display

Cheese always makes a nice complement to a bottle of wine. Serve with crackers and sliced party breads.

¼	pound of cheddar cheese
¼	pound Swiss cheese
1	2.2 ounce individual Brie cheese
6	fresh strawberries, washed
2	small bunches of grapes, washed

Dice cheese into bite-size cubes. Place cheese and fruit on a large plate and crackers and bread on a smaller one. *Doilies on plates will add an elegant touch.* Arrange grapes around cheese and fill in gaps with strawberries. Serve immediately or wrap and place in refrigerator to serve later.

The Art of Cheese Selections

Other delicious cheese varieties: Bel Paese, Boursin, Brie, Camembert, Cheshire, Colby, Edam, Fontina, Gouda, Havarti, Jarlsberg, Monterey Jack, and provolone, to name just a few. Cheeses come in soft, semisoft, semisoft to hard, blue-veined, to hard and very hard styles. Sharpness depends on aging process.

Yield: 2 servings

The Art of Garnish Touches

When serving appetizers don't forget to add special garnishing touches. A silver tray will always add a special touch.

A touch of paprika or chopped parsley can go long way towards making food look more elegant and appetizing. Also try lemon and lime wheels, lemon crowns, lemon wedges, fresh flowers, sprigs of fresh herbs, radish roses and designs cut out of vegetables.

Jumbo Lump Crabmeat Parfait

Fill two long-stemmed margarita glasses with lettuce and crabmeat, then garnish to create a delicious seafood parfait.

1	head radicchio lettuce
2	cups lettuce, shredded
⅔	pound jumbo lump crabmeat, checked for shells
2	lemon wheels
2	black olives for garnish
2	parsley sprigs for garnish
½	cup Mustard Sauce, *see page 194*
½	cup Cocktail Sauce, *see page 194*

In two large margarita glasses, place leaves of radicchio upright. Fill glass halfway with shredded lettuce. Fill remainder of glass with crabmeat. Garnish rim with lemon wheels and black olives. Top with parsley sprig. Place sauces in small ramekins on the side. Serve crabmeat parfaits and sauces on plates covered with doilies and cocktail forks.

Yield: 2 servings

Lamb Tips with Chutney, Curry, and Mustard

The local butcher will be glad to cut you some lamb tips. Mango chutney is the perfect compliment to lamb.

10	ounces lamb tips
1	tablespoon butter, melted
½	cup mango chutney
¼	teaspoon curry powder
⅛	teaspoon Coleman's prepared mustard
¼	cup blanched almonds, chopped
⅛	small head leaf lettuce
1	parsley sprig for garnish

In medium size sauté pan over moderate heat, sauté lamb in butter until done to taste.

In a small mixing bowl, combine lamb, chutney, curry powder, and mustard; mix well. Place mixture on medium size plate covered with leaf lettuce. Sprinkle almonds on top. Serve speared with wooden toothpicks. Garnish plate with parsley sprig and serve.

Yield: 2 servings

Escargot with Brie Butter in Mushroom Caps

Brie cheese complements the flavor of escargot, a favorite of mine.

10	large snails, canned
1	tablespoon butter
¼	teaspoon garlic, minced
2	tablespoons Pernod liquor
10	large mushrooms, cultivated
1	tablespoon lemon juice
2	lemon crowns for garnish, *see page 159*
2	parsley sprigs for garnish

Brie Butter

2	2.2 ounce individual Brie cheeses
2	tablespoons butter at room temperature
1	tablespoon chives, chopped

Radicchio Cole Slaw

2	small heads radicchio
2	tablespoons mayonnaise
1	teaspoon granulated sugar
1	tablespoon red wine vinegar

Snail preparation: Wash snails. In sauté pan, melt 1 tablespoon butter over moderate heat. Add snails, garlic and Pernod; sauté for 2 minutes, stirring constantly. Remove from heat and place to the side.

Brie Butter Preparation: Put ingredients for Brie Butter in food processor and blend, pausing to scrape down sides 3 or 4 times. Remove Brie Butter from food processor and place in small bowl. Refrigerate until ready to use.

Radicchio Cole Slaw Preparation: Cut bottoms off radicchio and wash their leaves. Hold radicchio leaves together and julienne into very thin strips. In medium size mixing bowl add mayonnaise, sugar, and vinegar; blend thoroughly. Add radicchio and toss

Mushroom and Final Preparation: Remove stems from mushrooms and wash caps. Place caps in large pot of boiling water, remove from burner, and let stand for 4 minutes. Remove caps from water and place in a baking pan. Place a snail in each mushroom cap. Heap ample portions of Brie butter over snails.

Bake in oven at 325° F for 7 to 9 minutes or until done. Remove stuffed caps and place five around edge of each plate. In middle of each plate, place a portion of radicchio cole slaw. Garnish with lemon crowns and parsley sprigs.

Yield: 2 servings

Oysters Rockefeller with Fresh Mozzarella

This is a good recipe for you to try if you don't like the taste of raw oysters. Spinach and a licorice-based liqueur (Pernod) enhance the flavor of the baked oysters.

½	pound spinach, fresh
3	tablespoons butter or margarine
1	teaspoon garlic, minced
¼	medium onion, chopped
½	lemon, squeezed for juice
1	ounce Pernod liquor
1	pinch salt and white pepper
12	oysters on the half shell
½	pound mozzarella, fresh
2	lemon crowns for garnish, *see page 159*
2	parsley sprigs for garnish

Preheat oven to 375° F.

Wash spinach, remove stems, and place leaves to the side.

Place butter, garlic, and onions in sauté pan over moderate heat. Cook onions until transparent. Add spinach, lemon juice, and Pernod. Seasoning with salt and white pepper to taste. Cook 1 to 3 minutes, or until spinach is limp, stirring continuously.

Drain liquid from oysters. Cover each oyster completely with spinach mixture. Place oysters on baking dish. Cover each oyster with a thin slice of fresh mozzarella. Bake 7 to 9 minutes or until oysters are hot throughout. Place oysters on two plates and garnish with lemon crown and parsley sprigs.

Yield: 2 servings

Santa Fe Eggplant Dip with Pita Wedges

A tasty favorite from the Santa Fe Grill restaurant.

1	medium eggplant
¼	medium onion, chopped
¼	tablespoon garlic, minced
¼	cup olive oil
2	tablespoon cilantro, chopped
2	tablespoon rice vinegar

¼   tablespoon lemon juice
1   pinch salt and pepper to taste
1   parsley sprig for garnish

Pita Bread Wedges
4   pieces pita bread
¼   cup butter, melted
½   tablespoon granulated garlic
1   tablespoon paprika

Preheat oven to 325° F.

Peel and slice eggplant. Brush eggplant and onion with olive oil and garlic. Place on baking pan and cook in oven for 8 to 10 minutes. Remove and place in food processor or blender and add cilantro, rice vinegar, and lemon juice and purée, stopping twice to scrap down sides with spatula. Place in small serving bowl.

Pita Bread Wedges: Cut pita bread in eighths to form triangles. Lay out pita triangles on baking pan and lightly coat with melted butter. Sprinkle with granulated garlic and paprika. Bake pita wedges in 350° F oven for 4 to 7 minutes or until pita is toasted and crispy. Remove from oven, serve warm.

Place Eggplant Dip in serving bowl in the middle of large size platter. Surround with toasted pita wedges and serve. Garnish plate with parsley sprigs or cilantro.

Yield: 2 servings

Showy Jumbo Shrimp Cocktail

The most popular shellfish is shrimp. Take advantage of contrasting colors in cocktail and mustard sauces *on page 194* when painting plates.

1   lemon, cut in half
2   tablespoons Old Bay seasoning
6   large shrimp, shelled, tail on and deveined
½   cup cocktail sauce, *see page 194*
½   cup mustard sauce, *see page 194*
2   lemon crowns for garnish, *see page 159*
2   parsley sprigs for garnish
2   large pitted black olives for garnish

In large saucepan, combine one lemon and Old Bay seasoning with one quart of water. Bring to a rolling boil. Add shrimp all at once; return to boil. Reduce heat and simmer covered 1 to 2 minutes, or until shrimp are cooked. Drain; place in ice bath to cool. Then refrigerate and keep covered, until ready to use.

Spread cocktail sauce in middle of plate. Use mustard sauce to create design on top of cocktail sauce. Circle shrimp around edge of plate. Garnish with lemon crowns, parsley sprigs, and black olives.

Yield: 2 servings

Smoked Salmon Eclairs with Vermouth

Quick Tip: You can purchase empty eclair shells used in this recipe from your local bakery.

2	large eclair shells, see below
⅔	cup cream cheese, room temperature
¼	pound smoked salmon, sliced thin
12	cocktail onions, drain juice
2	tablespoons capers
2	ounces dry vermouth
1	tablespoon lemon juice
2	lemon crowns for garnish, *see page 159*
2	parsley sprigs for garnish

Eclair shells

¼	cup boiling water
2	tablespoons butter
¼	cup all-purpose flour, sifted
1	large egg, unbeaten

Split shells in half. Fill eclair shells with cream cheese. Place eclair shell on one side of plate and let sliced smoked salmon hang off edge of eclairs. Place shell tops back on. On top of salmon, place onions and capers. Dribble vermouth on top. Garnish with lemon crowns, parsley sprigs and serve.

Preparing Eclair Shells: Preheat oven to 350° F. In a saucepan bring water to full, rolling boil. Add butter and stir vigorously until it melts. Then add flour all at once. Stir vigorously until mixture forms a ball in the center, away from the edges of the pan. Remove from heat and let cool 5 minutes. Place in electric mixer, add egg, and beat until mixture is very stiff.

Fill pastry bag with the batter mixture. Press out into oblong shape: 4½–inch long by 1–inch wide. Bake for 40 to 50 minutes or until well risen and crisp. Cool on a wire rack.

Yield: 2 servings

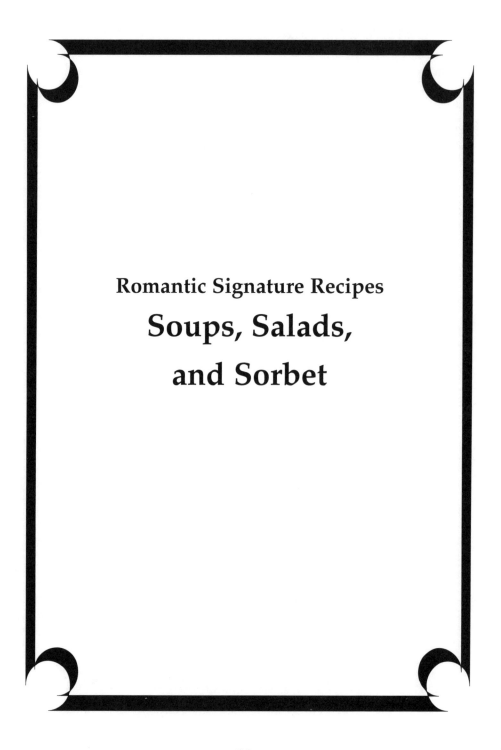

Romantic Signature Recipes

Soups, Salads, and Sorbet

The Soup, Salad, and Sorbet of a Relationship

Hot to the bone, crispy and crunchy, then the sorbet is sweet and chilling to the palate. Just like a relationship should be crispy, crunchy, sweet, and chilling – or are we talking about food?

Emotions That You Feel

A state of mind that controls emotions such as heart–driven, passionate, or gut reaction. Learn to share emotions, understand, and comprehend each other's wavelength

Different "S" Emotions

Different Counter reactions

Secretive = Open up and share

Shyness = Be bold and have fun

Sabotage = Understand and change

Sagacious = Fairness

Soup for the Soul

Soup is a good source of nourishment for the body and the spirit. Whether you make it at home or buy pre-made, there is a soup to meet everyone's taste and diet.

Soup Reminders

When making soups or just cooking, learn to use herbs and spices for added flavor. When using store-bought chicken broth, check labels for MSG and salt content.

Cream of Broccoli Soup

For cauliflower soup substitute cooked cauliflower for broccoli.

2	cups broccoli florets, cooked
1½	cups chicken consommé
2	tablespoons butter
2	tablespoons all-purpose flour
1	pinch thyme leaves
½	cup milk or light cream
1	pinch white pepper

In a blender or food processor, combine half of broccoli florets and ¼ cup of the chicken consommé. Cover and blend for about 20 to 30 seconds or until smooth and set to the side.

In medium saucepan, melt butter or margarine. Stir in flour, thyme, and white pepper. Mix to a smooth paste. Add milk or cream all at once. Cook until thickened and smooth, stirring constantly. Add broccoli mixture, broccoli florets, and remaining broth. Bring to a simmer, stirring constantly. Season to taste with white pepper.

Yield: 2 servings

I Love You Chicken Noodle Soup for the Soul

Perfect for when you're not feeling too good.

3	cups chicken stock, *see page 203*
¼	cup celery, diced
½	cup carrot, peeled and diced

¼	cup onion, diced
1	tiny pinch of thyme
¼	pound cooked chicken
¼	cup cooked pasta, chopped

Make chicken stock as shown *on page 203*. In saucepan over moderate heat add chicken stock, celery, carrots, onion, and thyme. Cook until vegetables are tender. Add chopped and cooked chicken and cooked pasta, then bring to a simmer. Serve with a warm smile and kiss on the forehead. And don't forget to say *I love you*.

Yield: 2 servings

Sherried Mushroom Bisque

Add a little zest to mushroom soup with sherry.

1	8 oz. cream of mushroom soup, canned
1	8 oz. chicken consommé, canned
¼	cup heavy cream
1	pinch nutmeg, ground
1	pinch cayenne pepper
2	tablespoons dry sherry

Combine all ingredients except sherry with ¼ cup water in medium saucepan. With a wire whisk, beat until well mixed. Over high heat, bring to a boiling, uncovered; stir occasionally. Reduce heat; simmer 5 minutes, stirring occasionally. Remove from heat. Stir in sherry. Serve at once.

Yield: 2 servings

Swiss Potato Leek Soup with Chives

The Swiss cheese will give a sharp, nutty flavor and body to this delicious potato soup.

3	cups chicken stock, *see page 203*
1	large Idaho potato, peeled and diced
1	tablespoon butter
¼	cup leeks, finely chopped
¼	cup onion, chopped
¼	cup heavy whipping cream

3	ounces Swiss cheese, grated
2	tablespoons chives, chopped
1	pinch white pepper to taste

In medium saucepan, add butter, leeks, and onion; sauté until onions are transparent. Add heavy whipping cream and simmer 5 minutes. Add potatoes and chicken stock. Simmer and stir until potatoes are soft. Place potato mixture in blender or food processor. Blend about 10 seconds or until smooth. Return to saucepan.

Add Swiss cheese. Stir until melted and blended in. Adjust flavor with white pepper. Simmer for additional 1 minute. Ladle the soup into individual serving bowls. Sprinkle chopped chives on top.

Yield: 2 servings

Wild Brandied Berry Yogurt Soup

A fast and easy soup that you can vary to suit your taste by using alternate fruits. Fresh melon, papaya, and kiwi are great fruits to use instead of berries.

2	cups plain yogurt
2	tablespoons honey
1	teaspoon lime juice
¼	cup blackberries
¼	cup raspberries
¼	cup strawberries
1	teaspoon brandy (optional)
2	mint leaves for garnish

Wash fruit and clean off stems as needed. Blend yogurt, honey, and lime juice in small bowl.

Place all but ¼ cup of yogurt mix in a food processor or blender. Blend until smooth. Serve at once or refrigerate until later. To serve, place fruit soup in bowls and using ¼ cup of yogurt mix, dribble on top of soup for color design. To garnish, place mint leaves on side of soup bowl.

Yield: 2 servings

The Art of Colorful Salads

When creating salads, remember that food should look appealing. Tomatoes should have a nice red color, oranges should be bright. Broccoli should have an even green color. Cauliflower should be clean and white. Even colors indicate a high-quality product.

For a successful salad, greens must be clean, fresh, crisp, cold, and well drained, or the salad will lack quality.

The quality and selection of produce has greatly improved over the years, so enjoy the abundance and have a salad today.

The Wonderful World of Lettuce

Few people realize the wonderful variety of lettuce available for salad preparation.

Belgian endive: Straight and slender leaves, perfect for show. A slightly bitter taste.

Bibb lettuce or Limestone lettuce: Smaller than Boston lettuce (cf. next) but has something of the same shape. A delicious flavor!

Boston lettuce: Tender and has velvety spreading leaves.

Curly endive: Twisted leaves varying from dark green at the edges to pale-yellow heart. Has a bitter tang.

Escarole: Leaves are broader than chicory and not as curly. They are dark green, edging into yellow.

Head lettuce or iceberg lettuce: A firm, tight, compact head of light green leaves.

Leaf lettuce: Crisp and has curly edge. Lovely green color and good flavor.

Oak lettuce: Deeply notched leaves which look like true oak leaves.

Radicchio: A red-leafed Italian chicory often used as a salad green. Firm leaves with a slightly bitter flavor.

Romaine lettuce: Long head and spoon-shaped leaves, coarser and crisper than head lettuce.

Spinach: Not a true lettuce, tender; and has a robust taste.

Watercress: Dark green in color; distinctive, tangy taste.

The Art of Salads

If you break lettuce up in bite-size pieces by hand and not a knife, it will stay fresh longer. Always serve salads in well-chilled wooden bowls or plates.

Always wash and thoroughly rinse salad greens; chill before serving. Vegetables should be washed before cutting.

The Art of Salad Painting

When I create salads, I think of the rim of the plate as a picture frame and the salad as a canvas on which you will create a work of art.

Garnish Suggestions

A touch of paprika or chopped parsley can go long way towards making food look more elegant and appetizing. Also try lemon and lime wheels, lemon crowns, lemon wedges, sprigs of fresh herbs, radish roses and designs cut out of vegetables.

Dressing Hint

Salad dressing should be added to greens just before serving.

Apple, Carrot, and Raisin Salad with Honey-Lime Yogurt

Use fancy-grade apples for best results. Yogurt is a great base for making sauces.

2	medium carrots, peeled and shredded
1	large red apple, cored and diced
¼	cup raisins
1	tablespoon parsley, chopped

Honey-Lime Yogurt Dressing

⅓	cup plain yogurt
2	tablespoons honey
½	lime squeezed for juice

Peel and shred carrot using grater. Place carrot in a large mixing bowl. Cut apple in half, core and dice in bite-size pieces. Add apples and raisin to mixing bowl and toss gently.

In a small mixing bowl blend yogurt, honey, and lime juice. Adjust flavor to taste. After mixing, add to carrots, apples, and raisins. Toss until coated thoroughly. Place mixture on serving plates and garnish with chopped parsley.

Yield: 2 servings

Bibb and Radicchio Salad with a Raspberry Dressing

Bibb lettuce is a favorite of mine to use when creating simple, elegant salads such as this one.

1	medium head Boston Bibb lettuce
1	medium head radicchio lettuce
¼	cup raspberry vinegar
¼	cup corn oil
½	small red pepper, diced

Wash Bibb and radicchio lettuce in ice water and drain thoroughly. Hold radicchio leaves together and slice into thin strips.

Prepare raspberry dressing by combining raspberry vinegar and corn oil in small bowl and blend thoroughly.

Place Bibb leaves on two salad plates and in the middle of plates place shredded radicchio in neat piles. Dribble with dressing when ready to serve. For color, sprinkle with diced red pepper. Serve excess dressing on the side.

Yield: 2 servings

Cucumber Salad with Dill and Vine-Ripe Tomatoes

Fresh dill will add a distinctive flavor. A nice hearty salad.

1	large cucumber, peeled
½	medium red onion, chopped
⅓	cup plain yogurt
2	teaspoons lemon juice
1	teaspoon fresh dill chopped
1	pinch salt and white pepper
2	medium vine-ripe tomatoes, cored, and sliced

Peel cucumber and cut in half lengthwise. Next, remove all seeds by scooping out insides. Cut crosswise into quarter moon shapes. Place cucumber and onions in large bowl. In small mixing bowl, beat together yogurt and lemon juice. Chop fresh dill, reserving 2 sprigs for garnish. Stir salt, white pepper, and dill into mixture. Pour yogurt mixture over cucumbers and onions. Place sliced tomatoes on two plates. Place cucumber dill mix on top and garnish with reserved sprig of fresh dill.

Yield: 2 servings

Grilled Portobello Mushrooms, Tomato, and Mozzarella Salad

Marinate and sauté portobello mushrooms to bring out their flavor.

1	large Portobello mushroom
¼	cup Vinaigrette Dressing with Capers and Herbs, *see page 197*
¼	pound fresh mozzarella cheese
2	slices vine-ripe tomato
2	slices yellow tomato
1	small head Bibb lettuce, washed
2	large basil leaves for garnish

Gently wash portobello. Cut mushrooms into slices lengthwise through entire stem and cap, about ¼-inch thick. Marinate in half of vinaigrette dressing for 30 minutes. Cook portobello mushrooms on a preheated grill on each side about 1 to 2 minutes over moderate heat. Place to the side. Slice tomatoes and wash lettuce. Place 1 slice each of red and yellow tomato on top of lettuce on salad plates with lettuce partly showing. Slice mozzarella into 4 slices. Place a slice of mozzarella and a slice of mushroom on top of tomato slices and repeat. Dribble with salad dressing. Garnish with basil leaves.

Yield: 2 servings

Herb-Blended Eggplant and Salad

For this recipe you will use a vinaigrette dressing.

¼	head red oak lettuce
¼	medium head radicchio
½	medium head Belgian endive
½	cup Vinaigrette Dressing with Capers and Herbs, *see page 197*
½	small eggplant
1	vine-ripe tomato, cored and cut into 6 wedges
¼	cup sliced black olives

Preheat grill or broiler to high heat.

Wash, separate, and chill lettuce leaves

Make vinaigrette dressing — *see page 197*. Peel eggplant and slice lengthwise into four ⅓–inch thick slices. Place in shallow baking pan and coat with half of vinaigrette dressing. Cook on grill or broiler, each side for 2 to 3 minutes or until it just starts to soften and brown.

Artistically place chilled lettuce leaves on plate. Add eggplant side-by-side on top of lettuce, with tomatoes and olives placed around edge of plate. Thoroughly mix vinaigrette dressing and dribble on salad and serve.

Yield: 2 servings

Newlywed Cherry Fruit Salad

This is a fun salad to feed each other!

½	cup fresh pitted sweet cherries
½	cup cantaloupe melon balls
¼	cup avocado, diced
½	cup sliced peaches
¼	cup Honey–Mustard Poppy Seed Dressing, *see page 196*
¼	medium head leaf lettuce

In mixing bowl, combine fruit and dressing, toss gently. Refrigerate 1 hour or until well chilled.

Before serving toss again and serve on a bed of leaf lettuce.

Yield: 2 servings

Honeymooners Hearts of Palm Salad

Hearts of palm should be soft, not hard. Ask for selection assistance at a gourmet market.

6	canned hearts of palm
½	small head Bibb lettuce
4	large jumbo green stuffed olives, sliced
½	medium red bell pepper, julienne, *see page 114*
1	tablespoon chopped parsley
1	pinch paprika, as needed
½	cup Honey–Mustard Poppy Seed Dressing, *see page 196*

Cut hearts of palm lengthwise into strips. Place half of washed and cut Bibb lettuce on serving plates. Arrange hearts of palm, stacked against each other in different directions. Add olives and red peppers. Top with chopped parsley.

When ready to serve, dribble Honey–Mustard Poppy Seed Dressing over plate; serve remaining dressing on side.

Yield: 2 servings

Passionate Crabmeat Salad

Try substituting crabmeat with shrimp salad as a delicious variation.

1	large ripe avocado
4	large strawberries, washed with stems removed
1	large kiwi, peeled and sliced
1	medium lime cut in wedges for garnish
2	parsley sprigs for garnish

Passionate Crabmeat Salad

6	ounces crabmeat
2	tablespoons celery, diced
¼	cup mayonnaise
¼	medium lemon squeezed for juice
½	tablespoon dill, chopped
1	pinch salt and white pepper to taste

Preparing Passionate Crabmeat Salad: Check crabmeat for shells. Place celery, mayonnaise, lemon juice, dill, and salt and white pepper in large bowl; mix well. Add crabmeat and toss.

Cut avocado in half and remove seed. Cut and peel skin off avocado. Slice avocado halves lengthwise into 4 wedges each. Using two salad plates, place a scoop of crabmeat salad on one side of each plate. On other side of plates, fan out avocado slices. Add strawberries and kiwis. Garnish with lime wedges and parsley sprigs.

Yield: 2 servings

Romeo Salad Bowl

Makes a tasty salad presentation!

½	small head Boston lettuce
1	ounce fresh spinach
1	small handful watercress, stems removed
½	small zucchini, washed
¼	medium onion, cut into thin rings
2	large mushrooms, sliced
1	medium vine-ripe tomato, cut into 6 wedges
6	medium pickled beets, julienne
½	cup Honey–Mustard Poppy Seed Dressing, *see page 196*

Wash lettuce and vegetables thoroughly. Slice zucchini thinly crosswise, using a knife or waffle cutter. Tear up lettuce and spinach. Place in large serving bowl. Top with remaining ingredients. Serve family style with dressing on the side.

Yield: 2 servings

Sweet Orange Salad with Grapefruit

Most lovers appreciate fresh fruit taste.

1	large orange
1	small grapefruit
¼	medium head lettuce, washed
¼	bunch watercress, washed
½	medium green pepper sliced in slivers
¼	small jar of pimentos
4	medium black olives, pitted
½	cup Fantasy French Dressing, *see page 195*

Prepare Fantasy French Dressing, following recipe *on page 195.*

Peel orange and grapefruit, cut into 6 slices each and set to the side.

Using a knife, slice lettuce into thin strips and place on sides of salad plates. Cut off watercress stems and place on top of lettuce. Lay fruit on plates, alternating between segments of grapefruit and orange. Garnish in between segments with green peppers and pimentos. Add black olives and serve with dressing on the side.

Yield: 2 servings

TriColor Arugula Salad with Lemon Dressing

Lemon and arugula combine to create a distinctive flavor.

Lemon Dressing

¼	cup corn oil
¼	cup lemon juice
½	medium lemon, peeled and grated
2	tablespoons sugar
1	pinch salt and white pepper to taste

2	ounces arugula lettuce
½	small head radicchio
½	small head Belgian endive
1	medium vine-ripe tomato
¼	cup sliced black olives

Lemon dressing: In a medium mixing bowl, combine corn oil, lemon juice, grated peel, sugar, and salt and pepper. Mix thoroughly and let sit in refrigerator 2 hours.

Remove stems from lettuce, wash completely. Cut Belgian endive ½–inch from stem and place 4 leaves on cold salad plates with tips facing outward. Next, pick 4 leaves of radicchio and place 2 each on salad plates to make a bowl in the middle of the plates. Place arugula in middle of bowl, flowing out slightly. Dice tomatoes and sprinkle on top of lettuce. Garnish with sliced black olives. Dribble a fourth of lemon dressing on top of salads when ready to serve. Serve extra dressing to the side.

Yield: 2 servings

Vine Ripe Tomato Shells Stuffed with Tangy White Tuna

A healthy, quick and easy appetizer – use white tuna only.

1	large vine-ripe tomato
¼	head leaf lettuce
4	ounces white tuna, canned
½	cup Vinaigrette Dressing with Capers and Herbs, *see page 197*
2	parsley sprigs for garnish
2	lemon wedges for garnish

Cut tomato in half and core out insides of each half keeping skin intact. Cover two small plates with leaf lettuce. Stuff each tomato shell with drained white tuna and place on top of lettuce.

Dribble a small amount of Vinaigrette Dressing with Capers and Herbs on top and serve excess dressing on side. Garnish plates with parsley sprigs and lemon wedges and serve.

Yield: 2 servings

Dancing Lemon or Orange Sorbet

Sorbet is simply frozen juice.

Lemon Sorbet

1½	cups lemon juice
¼	cup sifted powder sugar

Orange Sorbet
substitute orange juice for lemon juice

Place ingredients for sorbet in mixing bowl and stir until sugar is dissolved. Freeze 3 hours, stirring every hour while freezing. Do not let mixture freeze solid. If this happens, break up with a sturdy implement. Spoon mixture into a food processor and blend until light and fluffy. Serve in a bowls preferably garnished with fruit. Sorbet can be made and placed in freezer until ready to serve.

Yield: 2 servings

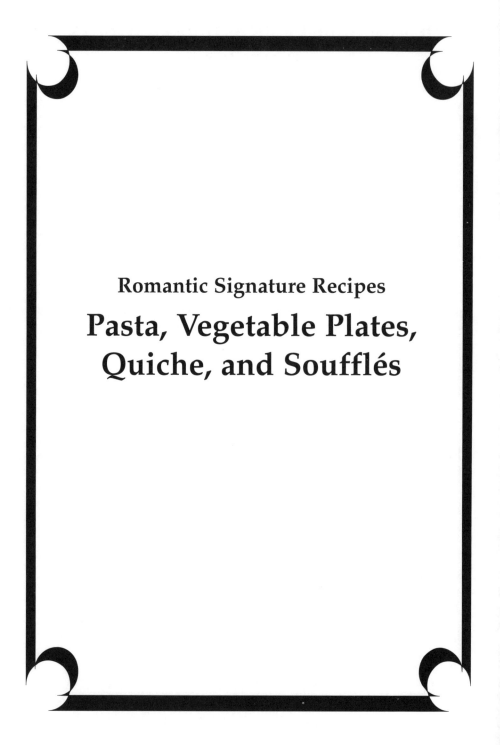

Romantic Signature Recipes

Pasta, Vegetable Plates, Quiche, and Soufflés

The Pasta and Vegetable Plates of a Relationship

Fulfilling, colorful, and a fad we have all had. Then it turns to a classic that is always so tasty. Every relationship should have the colors of life to look at and enjoy.

Colors of the Rainbow

A reflection of sunlight on drops that create a spectacular arc spectrum of colors. Read the colored layers and see your life.

The Rainbow Spectrum

Rainbow Colors Have Different Meanings.

Red = Physical
Orange = Emotional
Yellow = Mental
Green = Peace
Blue = Love
Purple = Aspirations
Violet = Inside You

Making Pasta Dough

Since fresh pasta is made from eggs, it must be used within a couple of days. Fresh pasta cooks in a fraction of the time required for dry pasta. Listed below is a basic recipe followed by a few simple variations. If you find that you enjoy making your own pasta from scratch, you may want to invest in a pasta press or machine. This will allow you to make many varieties of fresh pasta quickly and easily.

2	cups pasta, semolina or all-purpose flour
⅓	cup plus 2 teaspoons water
2	eggs at room temperature
2	teaspoons vegetable oil
½	teaspoon of salt

In a large bowl blend flour, water, eggs, and oil. Knead mixture to a smooth paste. (*See page 209* for kneading technique.) Cover the dough and allow it to rest for 45 minutes out of drafts.

Basil Pasta Dough: Add 1 tablespoon dry basil leaves to recipe above.

Black Peppercorn Pasta Dough: Add 1 tablespoon cracked black peppercorns to recipe above.

After dough has rested, dust work area with flour. Remove dough from mixing bowl and place on work area. Start to flatten out with a rolling pin. Flip dough over occasionally while rolling, and dust your work surface frequently. Continue rolling dough until it is about ⅛-inch thick or thinner. Spread the sheet of dough on a clean surface to dry. After drying, cut into strips or the shape desired with a sharp knife or pasta cutter.

Yield: 2 servings

Shaping Pasta Dough

There is a wide array of pasta-forming equipment available at specialty gourmet shops and by mail order. However, you can make the following varieties of pasta using minimal kitchen utensils.

Fettuccine and noodles: After rolling dough and letting it stand, cut into ¼-inch strips. Shake the strands to separate. For thin noodles, cut into 2-inch lengths.

Lasagna: After rolling dough, cut into 2½-inch strips. Cut into desired lengths.

Linguine or tagliatelle: After rolling dough and letting it stand, cut into ⅛–inch slices for linguine or ½–inch slices for tagliatelle. Shake the strands1 to separate.

Bow Tie: (Also called farfelle) Cut dough into 2 in x 1 in rectangles. Pinch the centers to form bow ties shapes.

How to Cook Pasta

The secret to cooking pasta is to use enough water and to make sure it is kept on a rolling boil all the way through cooking. Each pound of pasta requires 6 quarts of water, 1 teaspoon salt and 1 tablespoon of vegetable oil, and makes four servings.

Cooking Pasta: Bring water, salt, and oil to a rolling boil in a large pot with a lid. The oil prevents pasta from sticking together. Add one pound of pasta all at once. Cook fresh pasta for about 4 minutes, uncovered. Remove a piece near the end of cooking time and taste to determine if it is fully cooked. Most people prefer pasta cooked al dente - tender but firm - but this varies with taste. Keep pasta from sticking to bottom of pot while boiling by stirring occasionally.

Pasta Cooking Hint

Time the cooking of the pasta so it is just finished when needed to be added to the dish.

A normal serving is 4 ounces dry pasta per person. However, for someone trying to maintain or lose weight, a 2-ounce serving is recommended.

Jumbo Grilled Eggplant Raviolis with Red and Yellow Pepper Coulis

A colorful and delicious dish. Jumbo size ravioli are the key to this dish.

⅓	cup roasted red and yellow bell pepper coulis
10	ounces pasta dough, *see page 102*
2	slices eggplant, grilled
¼	cup ricotta cheese
1	egg wash
¼	cup olive oil
¼	tablespoon garlic, minced
¼	cup basil, chopped
2	fresh basil leaves for garnish

Prepare red and yellow bell pepper coulis, recipe follows. While roasting peppers, grill or roast the slices of eggplant.

Preparing Grilled Eggplant Raviolis: By hand or pasta machine, roll dough into four even squares ⅛–inch thick. On 2 squares, place grilled eggplant; layer with 2 tablespoons of ricotta cheese. Rub edges of pasta with egg wash. Carefully place other half of pasta sheets on top. Using fingers, press around each mound of filling. Seal edges of ravioli carefully, using the tip of a fork.

Place raviolis on a lightly floured cloth towel to dry for about 1 hour before cooking. In a large pot, bring water to a rolling boil. Add raviolis one at a time, cooking until edges are tender (about 5 minutes). Remove with a slotted spoon.

Add half of the olive oil to a large nonstick sauté pan and warm over moderate heat. When oil is hot, sauté each eggplant ravioli on each side for 1 minute. Sprinkle with garlic and basil while cooking. Remove and place on plates. Serve with red pepper coulis on one side and yellow pepper coulis on other side. Garnish with basil leaves and serve.

Yield: 2 servings

Red and Yellow Pepper Coulis

Sweet peppers are members of the bell pepper family. In this recipe, you will use both red and yellow bell peppers to make a Sweet Pepper Coulis.

½	each, roasted red and yellow bell pepper, *see page 105*
½	tablespoon shallots, minced
2	tablespoons red wine vinegar
¼	cup dry white wine
¼	cup heavy whipping cream
½	cup Chicken Velouté, *see page 200*
1	pinch of salt and white pepper to taste

Preparing Red and Yellow Bell Pepper Coulis: In medium size sauté pan over moderate heat, add shallots, vinegar, and white wine; reduce to about 1 tablespoon total. Add heavy cream and reduce in half. Finally, add velouté and simmer for 2 minutes.

In a blender, place half of the velouté mixture. Add roasted red pepper and purée for about 10 seconds. Place in a small pan to keep warm. Wash the blender and repeat the process with yellow pepper. If sauces are thin, reduce separately in saucepan over moderate heat until thickened.

Yields: ⅓ cup each coulis

How to Roast Peppers

Roast is a term used to describe a cooking method using dry heat, as in an oven or near a hot fire or coals. This will add an extraordinary flavor to peppers and allow you to remove their skins.

Blackening Peppers First: Sear 1 to 2 peppers over open gas flame or charcoal fire, or place under a broiler. Turn often until slightly blackened on all sides. When evenly blackened, place in a bowl and cover tightly with plastic wrap. Set to the side until cooled — 15 to 20 minutes. (Blacken skin of pepper only; do not burn inside flesh of pepper.)

Peeling peppers: Cut peppers in half. Remove stems and seeds. Lay halves flat, and using the dull side of a knife, scrape away skin and stray seeds. Cut peppers as needed for recipe.

Yield: 1/2+ cup

Pasta Rolls with Tri Color Julienne Vegetables

Use the sauces for painting the plate when creating this colorful and delightful dish.

Broccoli Pasta

10	ounces frozen broccoli, cooked
1	large egg
2½	cups all-purpose flour
3	tablespoons olive oil

2	tablespoons olive oil
1	tablespoon garlic, minced
1	carrot, julienne *see page 114*
1	zucchini, julienne
2	yellow squash, julienne
¼	cup basil, chopped fresh
1	pinch of salt and white pepper to taste
2	cups Tomato Basil Sauce, *see page 201*
1	cup Mornay Sauce, *see page 199*
2	large basil leaves for garnish

Preparing Broccoli Pasta: Drain 10 ounces frozen chopped broccoli, retaining purée. Put 1 large egg, at room temperature, in a blender. Mix in 2½ cups all-purpose or unbleached flour. Spoon broccoli purée into well. Add salt. Continue as with plain pasta *on page 102.*

Roll out broccoli pasta dough by hand or with a pasta machine ⅛–inch thick. Cut into 4 rectangles 6 x 5 inches. Let dry 20 minutes. Bring water and salt to a rolling boil in a large pot. Drop pasta rectangles one at a time into boiling water. Cook about 4 minutes. Carefully remove with a slotted spoon. Drain thoroughly on cloth towels. Place to the side.

In sauté pan, heat olive oil over moderate heat. Next add garlic, vegetables, and basil; saute 4 to 6 minutes, stirring constantly. Adjust flavor with salt and white pepper. Remove vegetables from stove and mix with a ½ cup of Mornay Sauce.

Take each rectangle, lay out flat and place hot cooked vegetables in each pasta rectangle. Roll up in jelly-roll fashion. Secure each roll with 2 toothpicks.

Place pasta rolls on baking pan coated with excess oil and cover. Bake in pre-heated 350°F oven for 5 to 7 minutes or until hot. Remove and using a spatula, carefully place two on each plate. Spread tomato basil sauce on sides and dribble with Mornay sauce. Garnish with basil leaves and serve.

Yield: 2 serving

Bow Tie Pasta with Broccoli and Sun-Dried Tomatoes

Another colorful and tasty dish. Sun-dried tomatoes and broccoli will combine to produce an intense flavor.

8	ounces bow tie pasta, *see page 102*
½	head broccoli florets, uncooked
¼	cup roasted garlic, *see page 114*
¼	medium onion, chopped
8	sun-dried tomatoes, julienne strips
⅓	cup olive oil
1	vine ripe tomato for concassé, *see page 114*
¼	cup fresh basil, chopped
1	pinch of salt and white pepper to taste
2	basil leaves for garnish

Prepare bow tie pasta following recipe *on page 102* and precook. Roast garlic, peel and leave cloves whole. Cook, peel, and dice tomato, using concassé technique *on page 114*. Set to the side for later use.

Prepare sun-dried tomatoes for use; follow the directions on their package (if dry, soak in hot water 30 minutes before cutting). Cut into julienne strips.

Add olive oil to large sauté pan and warm over moderate heat. Sauté broccoli and onion for 3 minutes before adding garlic, sun-dried tomatoes, and tomato concassé. Season with salt and white pepper to taste. Sauté for 3 additional minutes while stirring constantly.

Add bow tie pasta and chopped basil. Cook until pasta is hot. Place even amounts of pasta and sauce in two large bowls or plates. Garnish with basil leaves and serve.

Yield: 2 servings

Tagliatelle Pasta with Spinach and Pecan Pesto

Tagliatelle is ½–inch wide fettuccine shaped pasta.

1	batch tagliatelle pasta, *see page 102*
2	tablespoons olive oil
2	vine–ripe tomatoes for concassé, *see page 114*
2	basil leaves for garnish

Spinach Pecan Pesto

¾	cup olive oil
1	cup fresh spinach, chopped
¼	cup Parmesan cheese
1	tablespoon garlic, minced
2	tablespoons pecans
¼	cup fresh basil, chopped
1	pinch salt and white pepper to taste

Prepare Tagliatelle Pasta following recipes *on page 102.*

Preparing Spinach Pecan Pesto: Place oil, spinach, parsley, Parmesan cheese, garlic, pecans, basil, salt, and white pepper in blender or food processor. Cover and blend thoroughly about 45 seconds. If sauce is too thick, stir in 1 to 2 teaspoons hot water.

In large sauté pan, add 2 tablespoons olive oil and warm over moderate heat. Add tomato concassé and sauté 2 minute. Next add psto and sauté 2 minutes, constantly stirring.

Add tagliatelle pasta and cook until hot. Place an even amount of pasta and sauce in two pasta bowls or plates. Garnish with basil leaves and serve.

Yield: 2 servings

Grandma's Old-Fashioned Macaroni and Cheese

This budget-saver always brings smiles to faces!

3	quarts water
½	tablespoon vegetable oil
10	ounces elbow macaroni noodles
2	cups hot milk
1	tablespoon cornstarch
2	tablespoons butter or margarine
2	tablespoons grated onion
¼	teaspoon dry mustard
⅛	teaspoon Worcestershire sauce
1	small pinch white pepper
1	cup cheddar cheese, shredded
½	tablespoon butter or margarine
2	tablespoons bread crumbs
2	large tomato slices
2	parsley sprigs for garnish

In a large pot bring water to a full boil. Cook macaroni uncovered until tender but firm, stirring occasionally. Drain. Place in medium size casserole dish that is lightly greased with butter or nonstick spray.

In medium saucepan, blend cold milk and cornstarch. Add 2 tablespoons butter or margarine, onion, mustard, Worcestershire sauce, salt and white pepper. Bring to a boil over medium heat, stirring constantly. Reduce heat to low. Add cheese. Continue stirring until cheese melts. Pour mixture over macaroni. Melt ½ tablespoon butter or margarine in a small sauté pan, stir in bread crumbs, mix thoroughly. Sprinkle bread crumbs over casserole; place tomato slices on top. Set temperature at 350°F and bake 20 minutes or until golden brown and hot. Serve family style.

Yield: 2 servings

Jaded Oriental Vegetable and Tofu Stir Fry

Tofu is a soft textured soybean cheese that is readily available in supermarkets. Originating in the Far East, it has long been used as a staple of the Oriental diet. One of the great things about tofu is that, by itself, it is practically tasteless. However, it seems to have the ability to exhibit the flavor of whatever it is mixed with. Using tofu is a great way to add protein to items otherwise devoid of this nutrient.

½	cup celery, julienne *see page 114*
1	small carrot, julienne
1	each red and green bell pepper, julienne
¼	medium red onion, sliced
2	small shiitake mushrooms, sliced
¼	cup water chestnuts
¼	cup baby corn, canned
1	tablespoons sesame oil
8	ounces firm tofu, diced
½	tablespoon garlic, minced
1	teaspoon fresh ginger, peeled and diced
2	tablespoons vegetable oil
¼	cup soy sauce
¼	cup teriyaki sauce
¼	cup pineapple juice
½	tablespoon cornstarch
2	cups Seasoned Rice, *see page 188*
¼	cup green onion, chopped
2	scallion flowers for garnish

Cut the vegetables and place them to the side. To prepare sauce, in a mixing bowl, add vegetable oil, soy sauce, teriyaki sauce, pineapple, and cornstarch; mix thoroughly.

Add sesame oil to a hot preheated wok or large sauté pan. When the oil is hot, cook tofu, garlic and ginger about 3 minutes; remove with slotted spoon and place on plate. Next, add vegetables and cook, stirring constantly for 5 to 6 minutes. Add prepared sauce and simmer until it thickens and evenly coats vegetables. Place hot cooked rice on each of two plates to form large circles in which to place vegetables. Add vegetables and sauce, top with cooked tofu.

Garnish with green onions and scallion flowers; *see page 159* for directions. Serve at once.

Yield: 2 servings

Threes Company Omelette Supreme with Swiss and Avocado

Once you master this omelette, you will be creating others in minutes. You'll need an omelette pan. For a two or three egg omelette, a 7–inch nonstick pan is best.

For One Omelette

2 to 3	large eggs
1	pinch salt
1	pinch white pepper
1	teaspoon water
1	tablespoon butter or margarine

1	slice Swiss cheese
¼	ripe avocado, peeled and diced

For each omelette, break eggs into a small bowl. Add salt, white pepper and water. Beat just enough to mix yolks and whites. Place omelette pan over moderate heat. To the hot pan, add butter; heat until the foam begins to subside. Pour in egg mixture all at once. As soon as edge starts to turn opaque, slide spatula under and lift slightly, tilting pan so uncooked egg runs underneath. Gently shake the pan to keep the omelette from sticking. Continue lifting omelette and shaking pan until there is no more liquid and the top of the omelette looks moist and creamy.

Add Swiss cheese and avocados to omelette in a line with the pan handle. Holding the pan in your left hand, slide spatula under right edge of omelette; lift and fold over on top of ⅓ of omelette. Switch pan to your right hand and tilt over a warm serving plate. Gently shake the pan to slide unfolded edge of omelette onto plate. Flick your right wrist downward so that folded edge of the omelette, guided by spatula, falls neatly onto itself on plate. Garnish with fresh fruit and serve.

Repeat again for second omelette now that you are the omelette king or queen.

Yield: 2 servings

Whole Stuffed Eggplant with a Vegetable Casserole

In this recipe, you will prepare and stuff whole eggplants.

2	large whole eggplants
1	cup Béchamel Sauce, *see page 199*
2	tablespoons olive oil
1	tablespoon garlic, minced
¼	cup red onion, diced
½	cup carrot, peeled and diced
1	cup zucchini, diced
4	canned artichokes hearts
½	medium red bell pepper, sliced
1	cup bread crumbs
¼	cup Parmesan cheese, grated
1	large egg
¼	cup basil, chopped fresh
1	pinch of salt and white pepper to taste
2	cups Tomato Basil Sauce, *see page 201*
2	large basil leaves for garnish

Slice off stem ends of eggplant. Cook eggplants one at a time in boiling salted water in large covered pot for about 10 minutes. Lift out very carefully so as not to break skin. Cut a slice off the top and a thin slice off the bottom, so eggplant will cool. Remove most of pulp with a large spoon, using care not to break the shell of the eggplant. Chop ¼ of the pulp and set it to the side.

Preheat oven to 350°F. In sauté pan, heat olive oil over moderate heat and add garlic and onion. Sauté for 2 minutes or until onion is transparent. Next add carrots, zucchini, and two diced artichokes. Cook 3 minutes, remove and place in a large mixing bowl. Next, add chopped eggplant, ½ of the cream sauce, ¾ of bread crumbs, Parmesan cheese, egg and basil; adjust flavor with salt and white pepper. Mix together. Fill the eggplant with this mixture. Sprinkle bread crumbs on top. Cut remaining 2 artichokes in half and place them on top, along with slices of red pepper strips. Bake 25 to 30 minutes, or until stuffing inside of eggplant is fully cooked.

On two plates, carefully place the stuffed eggplants and surround with tomato basil sauce. Use an empty squirt bottle filled with strained cream sauce to create a simple design on top of tomato basil sauce. Garnish with basil leaves and serve.

Yield: 2 servings

Taco Crepes with California Vegetables in Mornay Sauce

Crepes are paper-thin pancakes that also have a wide variety of other uses.

4	crepe shells, *see page 227*
½	cup roasted red peppers, *see page 105*
2	tablespoons olive oil
1	tablespoon garlic, minced
½	head broccoli, cut into small florets
1	small carrot, julienne *see page 114*
¼	small head cauliflower, cut into small florets
½	cup dry white wine
1	cup Mornay Sauce, *see page 199*
2	large basil leaves for garnish

Prepare four crepe shells, following recipe *on page 227*.

In a food processor, purée roasted red pepper; set to the side for later use.

Heat olive oil in a large sauté pan over moderate heat. Add garlic, broccoli, carrots, and cauliflower. Cook 3 to 4 minutes, then add white wine and simmer until wine is almost gone. Add ¾ of Mornay Sauce to vegetables and simmer until vegetables are soft. Set extra sauce on low burner to keep warm

To serve, place one crepe shell on a serving plate and place ¼ of the vegetable-Mornay mix on one side. Fold over like a taco. Place second crepe shell on plate and fill. Repeat again on second plate. Pour remaining Mornay sauce on half of each crepe. Place red pepper purée on other half of crepe.

Garnish with basil leaves and serve.

Yield: 2 servings

Skyline Soufflé with Asparagus and Red Pimento

A soufflé is a light and airy entrée made from eggs yolks and stiffly beaten egg whites.

1	cup Mornay Sauce, *see page 199*
5	medium eggs
¼	cup unsalted butter

¼	cup all-purpose flour
1⅓	cups milk
1	teaspoon salt
⅛	teaspoon white pepper
1	teaspoon onion, finely grated
2	tablespoons red pimentos, chopped
¼	cup sharp cheddar cheese, grated
1¼	cup fresh asparagus, chopped fine
¼	teaspoon cream of tartar

Prepare Mornay Sauce following recipe *on page 199*. Set to the side for later use.

Separate egg yolks and whites. Place in separate mixing bowls. Let egg whites warm to room temperature.

Melt butter in medium size saucepan. Remove from heat and add flour. Stir in milk slowly and cook over low heat, stirring until mixture is smooth and thick. Add salt, white pepper, onion, pimento, and cheddar cheese. Stir until blended and set to the side to cool.

Preheat oven to 350°F. Grease a 1½ quart, straight–sided soufflé or casserole dish. Add asparagus to the cooled sauce.

In a separate bowl, beat egg yolks till thick and light. Blend in asparagus sauce. Combine warmed egg whites with cream of tartar. Using electric mixer set on highest speed, beat mixture until stiff peaks form when the beater is slowly raised.

Fold asparagus mix into stiff peaks of egg whites with a wire whisk or rubber spatula, using an under-and-over motion. Turn into prepared soufflé dish. Set in pan containing about 1–inch hot water; then bake 50 to 60 minutes. Serve with Mornay sauce.

Yield: 2 servings

Soufflé Hints and Tips

When making a soufflé, you must follow the recipe exactly and use the right size dish.

Do not open oven door while baking, or soufflé will fall. Check temperature with accurate thermometer after preheating oven. When the soufflé is done and ready to serve, the high crown will look dramatic and your entrance with the soufflé in hand will be impressive.

How to Roast Garlic

Garlic is a pungent bulb that is made–up of sections called cloves. There are many different ways to roast garlic. Here are a few methods I use.

Method One: Slice 2 to 3 whole garlic cloves in half with knife. Dribble with olive oil, wrap in tin foil, and place in preheated 350°F oven. Bake for 20 minutes or until lightly brown (check for doneness after 20 minutes).

Method Two: In sauté pan, warm olive oil over moderately high heat. Sauté peeled garlic cloves until they start to turn lightly golden brown, turning as you cook. Garlic should be crisp on outside yet soft in the middle.

Yield: ½ + cup

Tomato Concassé

Tomato Concassé is made with peeled tomatoes, diced, with seeds removed. The word concassé means to chop coarsely.

Preparing Tomato Concassé: Remove cores from 2 to 3 large vine-ripe tomatoes. Make X cuts on bottom of tomatoes using a sharp knife. Plunge the tomatoes into a saucepan of boiling water. Cook until skin begins to peel away, about 30 to 50 seconds, or longer if needed.

Remove tomatoes from saucepan and allow to cool. Peel off skins. Cut tomatoes in half and remove seeds, (if necessary run under cold water to wash out seeds). Cut tomatoes into strips, or dice.

Yield: about 1½ + cup

Julienne–Style Cutting

Cutting food products into uniform shapes and sizes is important to ensure even cooking and appearance.

Cut vegetables such as carrots and rutabagas into ¼–inch thick slices; then cut into 2½ to 3–inch strips. Vegetables such as peppers and leeks can be cut in half; lay them out flat and cut into strips.

Julienne=style cutting is the cutting of vegetables or fruit in (¼–in x ¼–in x 2½ to 3–in).

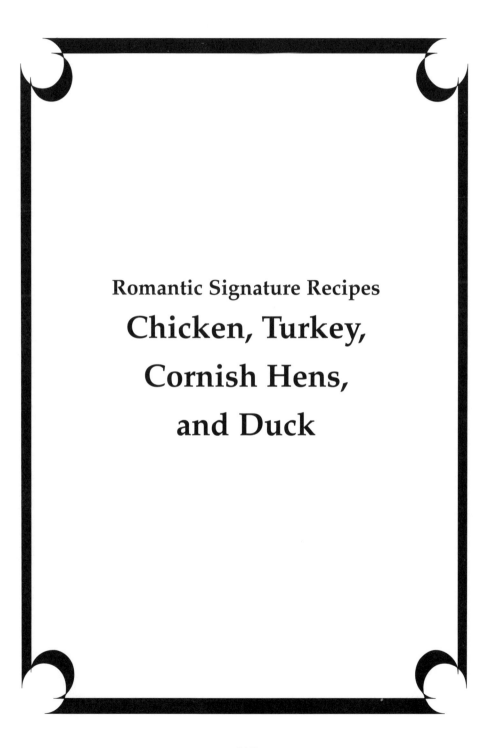

Romantic Signature Recipes

Chicken, Turkey, Cornish Hens, and Duck

The Wings of a Relationship

Have you ever had a dream that you can fly? What a feeling of invincibility and floating freely. In any relationship, each person should have the wings to fly and should support and help each other along the way.

Dreams vs. Responsibilities

Dreams are visions, fantasies, and figments of the imagination otherwise known as unconscious wishes. Responsibility is taking control of things you are responsible.

In Between Dreams and Goals

The Right Direction to Go
Obstacles to Get Through
How You Will Get There
Dreams = Visions to be Unleashed
Fear = A Powerful Emotion to Overcome
Responsibility = Answerable For
Goals = Aspirations Laid Out

Helpful Poultry Pointers

Chickens are classified by age and weight. Young chickens are tender and cook quickly; older chickens need more cooking to make them tender.

Broiler Fryers: Young chickens weighing from 1½ to 3½ pounds. Only 7 to 10 weeks old. Perfect for broiling, frying, and roasting.

Roasters: 4 to 6 pound chickens that are 16 weeks old. Great for roasting and rotisserie.

Capons: Young roosters that weigh 5 to 7 pounds

Stewing Hens: Adult chickens, 1 to 1½ years old. Weigh 4½ to 7 pounds. Use only for stocks, soups, and stews. Will need a lot of moist heat to tenderize.

Supermarket Varieties:

Whole Chickens: Consist of two breast halves, two thighs, two wings, and two drumsticks. They may be available already cut up.

Chicken Pieces: Sold as a variety of parts: Chicken legs, wings, and thighs.

Chicken Breast: A popular way to buy chicken because of its convenience. Also available boneless and or skinless.

Cornish Hens: Whole and available fresh or frozen, ¾ to 1½ pounds.

Turkey: Available fresh or frozen, 6 to 24 pounds. Turkey is like chicken and will come in a variety of cuts, even ground.

Duck or Duckling: Available fresh or frozen, 4 to 6 pounds. Whole, cut up, and boneless breast.

Pheasant: Available frozen, 2 to 3½ pounds.

Goose: Available fresh or frozen, 6 to 14 pounds.

Quail: Available frozen, fresh, and smoked, 4 to 6 pounds.

When buying poultry, plan on about ¾ pound per person. Plan on about ⅓ pound per person for boneless cuts.

Poultry should be used within 2 days of purchase or stored in freezer. Thaw poultry in refrigerator.

When ready to cook, wash poultry thoroughly under running water. Pat dry with paper towels. Giblets are usually packed inside whole birds and should be removed before rinsing.

Properly cooked poultry will be 180°F (80C) when checked with a meat thermometer. The tip of the thermometer should be inserted in the thickest part. If you don't have a meat thermometer, pierce the inner thigh with a fork. If the juices run clear and the leg moves easily, the poultry is cooked.

The internal temperature of stuffing must be 165°F before it is safe to eat.

Safety Precautions for Poultry

Special precautions must be used in the handling of raw poultry.

When handling raw poultry, everything that comes in contact must be kept clean. Wash chicken under running water. Always wash knives, cutting board, and hands before and after cutting chicken, to remove any bacteria. Poultry should always be completely cooked.

Flattening Chicken Breast Tips

Flattening chicken breasts will shorten cooking time and make chicken meat easier to chew.

Place one chicken breast between two sheets of heavy plastic wrap or waxed paper. Using the flat side of a meat mallet, empty wine bottle, or a small wooden cutting board, gently pound out chicken to desired thickness. Start from the center and work to the outside. Breasts are now ready for use in your recipe.

Trussing Poultry

Truss poultry to retain its shape during roasting. Butcher string should be twice the length of the bird to be trussed. Poultry skewers can also be used.

Using butcher string, wrap around tail and cross over legs. Wind string around legs; pull string toward center; cross ends of string. Pull string lightly to pull legs together. Pull ends of string along each side of breast. Turn bird over, grasp ends of string. Tuck wing tips under, pull string over wings. Pull string tightly around wings. Tie string securely and cut off ends. Turn breast side up. Use metal poultry skewers as necessary.

Almond Chicken with Orange–Basil Sauce

A sensational flavor combination! Easy to make and light.

1	2–pound broiler or fryer chicken, cut into 6 pieces
1	pinch salt and white pepper
3	tablespoons butter or margarine
2	tablespoons all-purpose flour
⅛	teaspoon cinnamon, ground
⅛	teaspoon ginger powder
1½	cups orange juice
¼	cup slivered blanched almonds
1	orange, peeled and cut into sections
2	tablespoons basil, chopped fresh
1	cup Seasoned Rice, *see page 188*
2	orange slices
2	large basil leaves for garnish

Wash chicken in cold water; pat dry with paper towels. Sprinkle with salt and pepper.

Brown chicken lightly in 3 tablespoons melted butter in large sauté pan over moderate heat. Remove chicken and set to the side. Mix flour, pinch of salt, cinnamon, and ginger. Blend into pan drippings to make a smooth paste.

Add orange juice and continue cooking, stirring constantly until sauce bubbles and thickens.

Return chicken to skillet along with almonds. Cover and cook over low heat for 30 minutes, or until chicken is fork tender.

Peel orange, cut into sections, and remove seeds. Add orange sections and fresh chopped basil to sauce and heat through. Serve chicken topped with small amount of sauce on a bed of Seasoned Rice. Garnish with orange slice and basil leaves. Serve the remaining sauce on the side.

Yield: 2 servings

Breast of Chicken Flambé with Brandied Cherry Sauce for Two

This delicious and romantic meal should quickly warm your mood for the evening!

2	8–ounce chicken breasts with bone and skin
1	ounce melted butter
1	teaspoon paprika
1	ounce brandy
1	pinch salt and white pepper to taste

Bing Cherry sauce

1	8 ounce can black bing cherries
2	tablespoons Burgundy wine
2	tablespoon sugar
½	teaspoon cornstarch
1	pinch salt

Preparing Bing Cherry Sauce: Drain juice from cherries. Combine juice with wine, sugar, cornstarch, and salt; mix thoroughly. Bring mixture to a boil until sauce thickens. Add the drained cherries.

Season chicken breast with salt, white pepper, paprika, and brush with butter. Bake for 30 minutes at 325°F or until cooked and tender. Place chicken in a medium size ovenproof serving dish and cover with sauce. Have table set, candles lit, all accompaniments on table, and turn off lights when ready to flambé.

How to flambé: Pour ¼ ounce of brandy over dish and place in middle of table. Using long wooden matches, ignite chicken breast. When flame goes out and liquor has burned off, you are ready to serve.

Yield: 2 servings

Caesar Chicken Breast over Fettuccine

If you like pasta and Caesar salad, you'll love this delicious chicken dish.

2	5 ounce chicken breasts, boned and skinned
¼	cup olive oil
¼	cup all-purpose flour
½	tablespoon garlic, minced
¼	cup dry white wine
2	tablespoons red wine vinegar

½	lemon, squeezed for juice
4	anchovy fillets
¼	teaspoon Worcestershire sauce
4	drops Tabasco® sauce
2	tablespoons fresh basil, chopped
1	cup Chicken Velouté Sauce, *see page 200*
8	ounce fettuccine pasta, precooked *see page 102*
2	lemon crowns for garnish *see page 159*
2	parsley sprig for garnish

Prepare and precook fettuccine pasta. Place chicken breast between two sheets of heavy plastic wrap and pound out lightly. *(See Flattening Chicken Breast Tips, on page 118)*.

Heat olive oil in a large sauté pan over moderate heat. Dredge chicken in flour and place in sauté pan. Cook on both side 3 minutes or until brown. Remove and place to the side.

Add garlic to sauté pan and cook until aroma of garlic is distinct, about 1 to 2 minutes. Add white wine and cook 1 minute additional. Add red wine vinegar and simmer 30 seconds more. Add lemon juice, anchovies, Worcestershire and Tabasco® sauces, basil and Chicken Velouté Sauce, bring to a simmer for 3 minutes.

Cut chicken breast into 8 strips, place in sauce, and cook for 3 minutes. Remove chicken and set to the side. Toss pasta with sauce. When hot, place onto serving plates. Place chicken strips on top of pasta. Garnish with lemon crowns and parsley sprigs. Serve.

Yield: 2 servings

Champagne Chicken with Shiitake Mushrooms

Champagne and Oriental mushrooms combine to add an exotic flavor to this delicious dish.

2	5–ounce chicken breasts, boned and skinned
2	tablespoons olive oil
¼	cup all-purpose flour
1	pinch of salt and white pepper to taste
1	tablespoon salted butter
2	tablespoons shallots, minced

3	ounces crimini oysters
3	ounces shiitake mushrooms
½	cup champagne
¼	teaspoon thyme, chopped
8	ounce fettuccine pasta, precooked *see page 102*
1	cup Chicken Velouté, *see page 200*
2	parsley sprigs for garnish

Prepare fettuccine pasta, following recipe *on page 102.*

Place chicken breast between two sheets of heavy plastic wrap and flatten to ¼–inch thickness. *(See Flatten Chicken Breast Tips, on page 118).*

Wash mushrooms thoroughly and cut in half. Heat oil in a large sauté pan over moderate heat. Coat chicken lightly with flour. Season with salt and white pepper. Place chicken in sauté pan and sear on both sides to a light brown. Remove chicken and place to the side.

In sauté pan, add butter, shallots and mushrooms. Sauté for 3 minutes. Away from heat add champagne and reduce in half. Add Chicken Velouté and simmer. Add chicken and thyme, simmer 5 to 6 minutes. Remove chicken and place on serving platters. Spoon sauce and mushrooms over top of chicken. Garnish with parsley sprigs and serve.

Yield: 2 servings

Chicken Francaise with Raspberry Mint Sauce

Chicken breast is coated with egg and Parmesan cheese then sautéed. A non-stick sauté pan will work wonders.

1	large egg
1	tablespoon Parmesan cheese
½	tablespoon parsley, chopped fresh
2	5 ounce chicken breasts, boned and skinned
¼	cup all-purpose flour
2	tablespoons oil for sautéing
1	tablespoon shallots, minced
¼	cup dry white wine
¼	cup raspberry vinegar
½	lime, squeezed for juice
¼	cup fresh raspberries, chopped
1	tablespoon salted butter

½   cup heavy cream
1   tablespoon mint leaves, chopped
2   sprigs mint leaves for garnish

Preparing Francaise Mix: Break eggs into a small mixing bowl and whip. Add Parmesan cheese and parsley. Whisk thoroughly.

Place chicken breast between two sheets of heavy plastic and flatten to ¼–inch thickness.

Heat oil in a large sauté pan over moderate medium heat. Flour chicken and dip in Francaise mix, coating thoroughly on all sides. Place chicken in sauté pan and cook on both sides until egg starts to lightly brown and chicken is cooked. Remove chicken and place to the side. Drain oil from pan.

In sauté pan, add butter and shallots; cook until shallots start to simmer. Add white wine, raspberry vinegar, and lime juice. Cook over low heat until reduced in half. Add heavy cream and reduce until sauce is really thick. Add fresh raspberries and mint , mix thoroughly. Add chicken, simmer until chicken is cooked and sauce thickens. Remove chicken and place on serving platters. Pour raspberry sauce over chicken breast. Garnish with mint leaves and serve.

Yield: 2 servings

Honey Roasted Half Chickens

Easy way to cook half chickens. Honey will caramelize to add a great flavor.

1   2½–pound whole roasting chicken, split in half
2   tablespoons salted butter, melted
½   tablespoon paprika
1   pinch salt and white pepper
½   cup honey

Split whole chicken in half down back and breast. Wash under running water. Place chicken halves on baking pan and brush with butter; sprinkle on paprika, salt and white pepper. Place in preheated oven at 350°F and bake 30 minutes. Remove from oven and brush with honey. Place back in oven and bake 20 more minutes until chicken is done. Brush lightly with extra honey before serving.

Yield: 2 servings

Classic Chicken Marsala with Fresh Mozzarella

This classic dish is seasoned with an extra twist of fresh mozzarella cheese.

2	tablespoons unsalted butter
1	tablespoon vegetable oil
2	6 ounce chicken breasts, boned and skinned
4	slices fresh mozzarella cheese
8	capers, drained
1	tablespoon shallots, minced
¼	cup Marsala wine
¼	cup heavy whipping cream
1	pinch of salt and white pepper to taste

Heat butter and oil in large sauté pan over moderate heat until melted and bubbly. Dredge chicken in flour seasoned with salt and white pepper. Add to sauté pan and reduce heat to medium. Cook uncovered 5 to 6 minutes per side until chicken is tender and golden brown. Remove chicken with slotted spatula to work surface. Top each chicken piece with a slice of fresh mozzarella, four capers and one anchovy fillet.

Return chicken to sauté pan, cover and cook over low heat for 3 minutes or until cheese is melted and juices from chicken run clear. Remove chicken and place on serving plates. Keep warm.

In sauté pan, add shallots to drippings remaining in pan, stir over medium heat for 30 seconds. Add Marsala wine and stir, cooking until reduced, about 1 to 2 minutes. Scrape up any brown bits in skillet.

Stir in cream and cook until sauce reduces and thickens slightly. Add salt and white pepper to taste. Spoon sauce over chicken. Garnish as desired.

Yield: 2 servings

Curried Chicken Breast with Fried Banana

Curry is a blend of spices that has a Middle Eastern flavor. Fried banana is so yummy.

2	6–ounce chicken breast, boned and skinned
1	pinch salt and white pepper to taste
3	tablespoons vegetable oil
1	teaspoon garlic, minced
1	medium onion, diced
1	small tart apple, peeled and diced
½	tablespoon tomato paste
½	tablespoon all-purpose flour
1	tablespoons curry powder
1	cup coconut milk
1	banana, peeled
¼	cup all-purpose flour
2	large eggs, beaten
¼	cup coconut, shredded
2	canned apricot halves
6	maraschino cherries, chopped
1	tablespoon shredded coconut
2	large mint leaves for garnish

Season chicken with salt and white pepper. Heat oil in a large sauté pan over moderate heat. Sauté chicken until golden brown on all sides and remove with a slotted spoon.

Add garlic, onions, and diced apple. Sauté onion until transparent. Stir in tomato paste, flour, and curry powder. Cook for 1 more minute.

Gradually add coconut milk. Continue cooking, stirring constantly, until mixture thickens and comes to a boil. Return chicken to sauté pan. Cover, reduce heat, and simmer 15 to 20 minutes, or until chicken is tender.

While chicken is cooking, peel and slice 1 banana. Dip in flour, then in lightly beaten egg, drain off excess egg. Dip in shredded coconut. In separate pan with butter or margarine, sauté banana and apricot until golden brown all over. Remove with slotted spoon and place aside.

Serve chicken breast with fried banana and apricot on top. Garnish with maraschino cherries, shredded coconut, and mint leaves.

Yield: 2 servings

Ginger Chicken with Grape, Peanut, and Yogurt Topping

Ginger chicken cooked with grapes, peanuts, and yogurt sauce makes a light, refreshing, and romantic dinner.

2	9–ounce chicken breasts, quartered
¼	pound green grapes, seedless
1	cup plain yogurt
¾	tablespoon cornstarch
1	tablespoon ginger root, peeled and chopped
¼	cup roasted peanuts, chopped
1	pinch of salt and white pepper to taste
2	parsley sprigs for garnish

Preheat the oven to 350°F.

Place two washed and drained chicken quarters into a large ovenproof casserole dish. Sprinkle with ginger, salt, and white pepper. Cut grapes into halves and remove their seeds. Scatter grapes over the chicken. Add 1 cup water. Bake until the chicken is cooked, about 30 minutes.

Remove the chicken and grapes to a warm serving dish.

Pour yogurt into a small mixing bowl and stir in cornstarch. Put most of the chopped roasted peanuts in mixing bowl and slowly pour the liquid from the casserole into the yogurt, mixing well. Place the yogurt and peanut mixture in saucepan and cook over low heat, stirring constantly, until the sauce is thickened. Season the sauce with salt and pepper and pour it over the chicken. Sprinkle remaining peanuts on top and serve immediately. Garnish and serve

Yield: 2 servings

Honey–Mustard Chicken with Melon Balls and Kiwi

In this recipe, you should use a melon baller to prepare the fruit.

2	6–ounce chicken breasts, boned and skinless
¼	cup Dijon mustard
¼	cup brown mustard
¼	cup honey
3	tablespoons light cream
1	pinch salt
1	pinch white pepper
1	tablespoon salted butter
½	medium cantaloupe
½	honeydew melon
1	medium kiwi
2	tablespoons mayonnaise
2	large mint leaves as garnishes

Combine both mustards, the honey, cream, and salt and white pepper in a medium bowl and mix well. Next, spoon half of the mustard sauce into a glass mixing bowl. Set remainder aside.

Roll chicken in mustard marinade in the glass bowl, turning to coat completely. Cover and refrigerate for 30 minutes.

Heat butter in a large skillet over moderate heat until foamy. Remove chicken from the mustard marinade, shake off excess liquid and discard remainder. Place chicken in skillet and cook for 5 minutes on each side, or until chicken is well browned and no longer pink in the center and juices run clear.

To prepare melon balls, cut melon in half and remove seeds with a spoon. Prepare 2 cups of melon balls by scooping out equal amounts of flesh from each melon. Use a melon baller for this task (*you can also use a ½-teaspoon measuring spoon if a melon baller is not available*). To prepare kiwi fruit, peel and cut into thin slices. Set fruit aside.

Slice chicken breasts crosswise against grain and fan out on serving platters, set to the side.

Place reserved mustard sauce in small saucepan. Whisk in mayonnaise and heat thoroughly, using moderate heat. Drizzle some mustard sauce over chicken breasts. Add melon balls and kiwi, garnish with mint leaves; hand pass the remaining sauce.

Yield: 2 servings

Lonnie's Shrimp, Chicken, and Artichoke Casserole

This is one of my favorites!

8	ounces cooked chicken breast, diced
½	pound baby shrimp, cooked and cleaned
8	artichoke hearts, drained and cut in half
10	mushrooms, sliced
½	tablespoon salted butter
1	teaspoon Worcestershire sauce
¾	cup Béchamel Sauce, *see page 199*
2	tablespoons sherry
1	tablespoon Parmesan cheese
¼	teaspoon paprika
1	pinch of salt and white pepper to taste
1	cup seasoned rice, *see page 188*

Arrange artichoke hearts in bottom of small, shallow, buttered casserole dish. Add shrimp and chicken. Sauté mushrooms in butter and add to Béchamel sauce. Add Worcestershire, sherry, salt, and white pepper to white sauce. Stir gently and pour over casserole. Sprinkle with Parmesan cheese and paprika.

Bake uncovered at 350°F for about 25 to 30 minutes or until bubbly. Top should be brown. Garnish with parsley. Serve with your favorite rice.

Yield: 2 servings

Pecan Chicken with Praline, Apricot, and Chutney Sauce

Pecans, apricot, and chutney all complement each other. Praline liquor has a nutty, sweet, pecan flavor that is great to cook with.

2	5–ounce chicken breasts, boneless and skinless
¼	cup pecans, fine ground in food processor
1	tablespoon coconut, shredded

Praline, Apricot, and Chutney Sauce

2	tablespoons honey
1	fresh apricot, halved and pitted
¼	cup mango chutney
2	tablespoons mayonnaise

2	tablespoons praline pecan liquor
1	tablespoon Dijon mustard
1	pinch black pepper

Preparing Praline, Apricot,and Chutney Sauce: In blender, place honey, apricot, chutney, mayonnaise, praline liquor, Dijon mustard, and just a pinch of black pepper. Purée until smooth. In two mixing bowls, place sauce divided into ⅓ and ⅔ thirds.

Flatten chicken breast to ¼–inch thickness, *(See Flattening Chicken Breast Tips, on page 118).*

Dip chicken in ⅓ of sauce in mixing bowl and roll in ground pecans, shaking off excess. *(Discard sauce after dipping raw chicken in it.)* Arrange coated chicken in a lightly greased baking pan. Bake in preheated 325°F oven for 15 minutes, or until chicken juices run clear.

Place chicken breasts on two plates and dribble with excess sauce. Garnish as desired.

Yield: 2 servings

South Beach Chicken with Artichokes and Roasted Red Pepper

This "Yuppie Yardbird" is tasty beyond your wildest dreams.

2	6–ounce chicken breasts, boned and skinned
4	artichoke hearts, quartered
1	large red bell pepper, roasted, *see page 105*
8	leaves fresh basil
2	slices mozzarella cheese
¼	red onion, chopped
8	sun-dried tomatoes, softened in hot water
2	tablespoons pine nuts
¼	cup dry white wine
1	8–ounce can chicken consommé
¼	cup basil leaves, chopped

Place chicken breasts between two plastic sheets and using mallet, flatten to ¼–inch thickness. *(See Flatten Chicken Breast Tips, on page 118).*

In middle of pounded chicken breast, place equal amounts of artichoke, roasted red pepper, mozzarella, and basil leaves. Roll up chicken from short end like a burrito. Secure with wooden toothpicks.

Melt butter in large skillet over medium high heat until foamy. Add chicken and sauté until golden on all sides. Remove chicken, set to the side.

Add shallots, chopped onions, and sun-dried tomatoes. Cook over moderate heat for about 2 minutes. Add wine, cook 2 minutes. Add chicken consommé and bring to a simmer.

Return chicken breasts to sauté pan. Cover and simmer 15 to 20 minutes, or until tender, turning once basting often with sauce. Place chicken on plates, add fresh chopped basil to sauce and pour sauce over chicken. Garnish as desired and serve.

Yield: 2 servings

Chicken Stew in a Pastry Shell

Puff pastry dough can be bought at the store ready-frozen.

2½	pound stewing chicken, cut in serving-size pieces
2	ounces butter or margarine
2	celery stalks, diced in large pieces
¼	cup carrot, peeled and diced
¼	medium onion, chopped
¼	cup green peas
½	lemon, quartered
3	whole black peppercorns
1	small bay leaf
1	pinch salt
2	tablespoons all-purpose flour
2	puff pastry shells
1	pot boiling water as needed

Prepare pastry shells using Making Your Own Pastry Shells techniques which follows.

Wash chicken pieces thoroughly; pat dry with paper towels.

Melt butter in large pot over moderate heat, brown chicken pieces on both sides. Remove from heat.

Add celery, carrot, peas, onion, lemon, black peppercorns, and bay leaf to chicken. Add sufficient boiling water to cover chicken completely and bring to a boil. Reduce heat, covered, and simmer for about 45 minutes. Add salt; continue simmering, cover, about 1 hour, or until chicken is tender. Remove from heat. When fat forms on the surface, skim it off, reserving 2 tablespoons. Heat chicken fat in medium saucepan; remove from heat. Add flour, stirring to make a smooth paste. Remove chicken and vegetables with a slotted spoon and place to the side. Add roux to one cup chicken juice only; simmering until smooth. When sauce is smooth and thickened add chicken and vegetables and bring to simmer. Serve chicken and gravy in large pastry shells.

Yield: 2 servings

Making Your Own Pastry Shells

You will find many uses for freshly made pastry shells in addition to the recipe *on page 131.*

Lay frozen puff pastry on work surface. Cut into two 4 x 5 inch rectangles. Place pieces 3–inches apart on cookie sheet. Using paring knife, slice a rectangle ¾–inch inside perimeter of each shell, cutting only halfway through. Refrigerate for 30 minutes. Preheat oven to 450°F Carefully brush top of each pastry with a mixture of egg yolk and 1 teaspoon cold water. *(Do not let egg yolk mixture run down sides of rectangles or shells will not puff.)*

Bake in preheated oven at 375°F until the edges rise, about 12 minutes; then reduce temperature to 325°F and bake an additional 15 to 20 minutes, or until shells are a golden brown.

With a sharp knife, carefully cut around center section, removing tops. Scoop out any uncooked pastry in center. Return shells with tops to oven and bake for 3 minutes additional. Place to the side until needed.

Yield: 2 servings

Turkey-Broccoli Fried Rice

Quick and easy and will fill you up, yet inexpensive to make.

2	tablespoons sesame oil
½	tablespoon garlic, minced
¼	medium onion, chopped
¼	green pepper, chopped
1	cup Seasoned Rice, cold, *see page 188*
1	cup celery, chopped
1	carrot, julienne *see page 114*
8	mushrooms, sliced
¼	cup water chestnuts
8	ounces cooked turkey, cut in bite-size pieces
1	large egg, beaten
2	tablespoons soy sauce
4	cherry tomatoes, quartered
¼	cup green onions, chopped
¼	tablespoon sesame seeds

Heat a wok or large sauté pan over moderate high heat. Add oil, garlic, onion, and pepper. Cook until onion is transparent and the aroma of garlic is in the air. Sprinkle in rice. Stir until rice is coated with oil.

Add vegetables and cook, stirring for 3 to 4 minutes (vegetables should be tender but crisp). Stir in turkey and cook until heated throughout. Move mixture to the sides of pan. Pour in egg and cook until just set. Add soy sauce and tomatoes. Mix all ingredients thoroughly into rice. Serve on plates garnished with green onions and sesame seeds.

Yield: 2 servings

Turkey Cutlets with Lime Cream Sauce

The flavor of lime will add a nice taste.

2	6–ounce turkey cutlets
½	cup all-purpose flour
1	pinch of salt and white pepper
2	tablespoons olive oil
2	tablespoons shallots, minced
½	cup dry white wine
2	limes, squeezed for juice
½	cup heavy cream

1   tablespoon basil, chopped

Place sliced turkey cutlets between two sheets of plastic wrap and lightly flatten to ¼-inch thickness, *(See Flattening Chicken Breast Tips, on page 118)*.

Heat oil in large sauté pan over moderate heat. Dredge turkey in flour and season with salt and white pepper. Place cutlets in heated sauté pan and cook, uncovered, 3 to 4 minutes per side, or until turkey is brown and tender. Remove cooked turkey cutlets with slotted spatula to work surface.

Add chopped shallots and sauté for 1 minute. Add white wine and reduce to half. Add lime juice and cook for additional 30 seconds. Add heavy cream and scrape up any brown bits in skillet. Continue to reduce until sauce starts to thicken.

Return turkey cutlets to sauté pan. Sprinkle with basil. Cover and cook over low heat for 3 minutes or until turkey cutlets are done. Remove turkey and place on serving plates. Keep warm. Spoon sauce over turkey. Garnish as desired.

Yield: 2 servings

Turkey Meatloaf with Apricot Glaze

We all have had mom's meatloaf, so now is the time to make your own using turkey instead.

1   large egg
¼   cup milk
1   cup soft white bread crumbs
¼   teaspoon salt
⅛   teaspoon white pepper
1   teaspoon marjoram
1   pound ground turkey meat
1   teaspoon garlic, minced
¼   medium onion, chopped
¼   medium green bell pepper, chopped

Apricot Glaze
½   cup apricot jam
1   teaspoon lemon juice

Preheat oven to 350°F.

In large bowl, beat egg slightly with fork. Stir in milk, bread crumbs, salt, white pepper and marjoram. Add turkey meat and vegetables, knead well.

Shape mixture into 2 individual loaves. Place in baking pan and for bake 30 minutes.

Preparing Apricot Glaze: Combine apricot jam and lemon juice in small bowl and mix well.

Brush top of turkey loaf with glaze and bake for an additional 10 minutes. Remove turkey, slice loaves, and place on two plates. Dribble meatloaf with extra glaze. Garnish and serve.

Yield: 2 servings.

Rock Cornish Hens and Herb Blend

This classic recipe will be a big hit.

2	1 pound size rock cornish hens
1	clove garlic
2	teaspoons dried thyme
½	teaspoon seasoning salt
¼	teaspoon salt
¼	teaspoon white pepper
½	cup butter or margarine, melted
¼	cup lemon juice
¼	teaspoon paprika
¼	cup apricot marmalade

Preheat oven to 375°F.

Season inside of each hen with 1 split garlic clove, 1½ teaspoons thyme, ¼ teaspoon seasoning salt, ¼ teaspoon salt and ⅛ teaspoon white pepper. Truss hens, (*see Trussing Poultry, page 118*). If necessary, bring skin over neck opening and fasten to back with wooden toothpick or safety pin. Bind legs with string. Bend wings under bird.

Prepare basting sauce: Combine ½ cup butter with lemon juice, paprika, and remaining white pepper and thyme; stir well.

Heat some of the remaining butter in a medium skillet. Brown hens, turning and adding more butter as needed, to brown well on all sides.

Arrange hens in bottom of large roasting pan without rack. Brush well with basting sauce and roast, basting several times with sauce, about 40 minutes, or until nicely browned and done and temperature reads 180°F on meat thermometer. Serve with white or wild rice.

Yield: 2 servings.

Roasted Duck with Orange and Cherry Sauce

The duck is first roasted to brown the skin and melt away some of the fat, and then braised with cherries and orange juice. A goose of approximately equal weight may be substituted using this recipe.

1	2½ pound duckling, ready-to-cook
3	medium oranges
½	medium onion
1	small clove garlic
1	teaspoon salt
3	whole black peppercorns
8	ounces black bing cherries
⅔	cup canned chicken consommé
¼	cup orange marmalade

Preheat oven to 400°F.

Stuff duckling cavity with 1 orange quartered, onion, garlic, salt, and peppercorns. Truss duck (*see Trussing Poultry, page 118*).

Place duck, breast side up, on rack in a shallow roasting pan. Prick the skin all over with a fork to allow the fat to drain. Rub the skin with salt. Roast the duck, uncovered, for 1 hour.

Place pitted cherries into a large bowl. Add grated rind of 1 orange and juice of 2 oranges to the cherries.

When the duck has cooked for 1 hour, drain off the fat that has collected in the roasting pan. Remove the rack and return the duckling to the pan. Pour the cherries and orange juice around the duck with cup of chicken consommé. Cover the pan with foil and roast for 40 additional minutes. Insert meat thermometer into thigh. It should read 180°F when done. Remove the duck to a warmed serving platter. Drain half of the cherries and place them around the duck.

To prepare the sauce, place remaining cherries into a blender along with the cooking liquid and orange marmalade; then blend until smooth. Reheat the sauce, season to taste with salt and pepper, and serve on the side.

Remove poultry pins or twine. Carve duck into serving-size pieces, if desired.

Yield: 2 servings

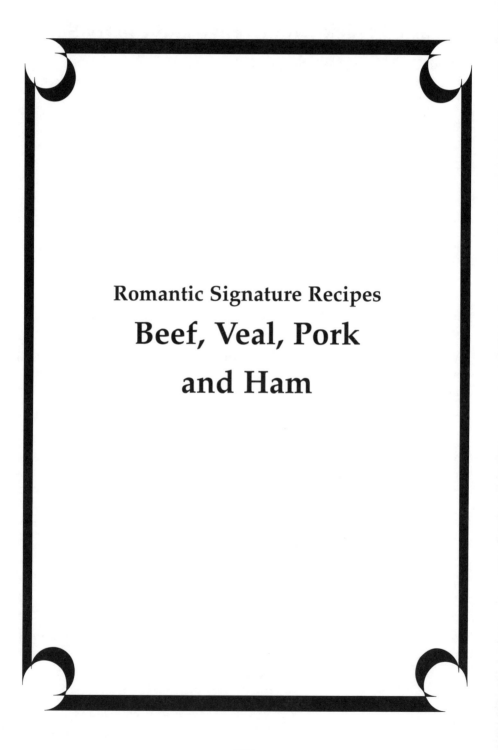

Romantic Signature Recipes

Beef, Veal, Pork
and Ham

The Stability of a Relationship needs Four Legs to Stand on.

Every relationship needs stability of four legs to stand on in order to build a stage on which to act on.

Stability

Balance is the key to distributing the feeling of being secure, a brace with which to stand on.

Four Legs of Stability

Build your own stage on which to express ones feelings.

1-Trusting in Each Other
2-Communicating With Each Other
3-Understanding of Yourself and Partner
4-Commitment to Each Other.

Then the ground work will be laid out to stand on.

Meat Varieties

There are many different ways of butchering beef. Techniques vary not only from country to country but also from region to region.

The smart thing to do is consult with your local butcher before making a purchase. He or she is always the best source of information.

Cooking Methods used for different cuts of beef

Cooking Guide: Round Steak (Braise) • Rolled Rump (Braise) • Sirloin Steak (Broil) • Porterhouse Steak (Broil) • Club Steak (Broil) • Tenderloin Filet from Filet Mignon (Broil) • Tenderloin from Loin (Roast) • Standing Rib (Roast) Rib Steaks (Broiled or Grilled) • Rolled Rib Roast (Roast) • Chuck Steak (Broil) • Round - Bone Pot Roast from Chuck (Braise) • Blade - Bone Pot Roast from Chuck (Braise) • Boston Cut from Chuck (Braise) • Shank (Braise; Simmer for Soup) • Cut from Plate (Simmer; Braise) • Short Ribs (Braise)• Brisket (Simmer, Corned or Fresh) • Flank (Braise; Broil).

Beef Hints

The leanest cuts of beef are Top Round Steak, Sirloin Steak, Top Loin Steak, Tenderloin, Eye of Round, Bottom Round and Chuck. And these will contain the least fat and cholesterol.

When purchasing ground beef, select the leanest variety available. You will recover the price difference when you drain the fat as you cook, and will serve healthier meals.

Go Beyond Beef!

There other kinds of steaks, as well as chops and cutlets, that can be cooked by dry heat in a skillet or under a broiler. Ham, pork, lamb, veal, and game steaks or filets are also available.

Veal Hint

As the price of veal has risen, fewer people buy veal because they assume it is too expensive. However, when serving veal cutlets you need only about ¼ pound per person. Even if veal costs $10.00 per pound, it will cost only $2.50 per portion, which many consider reasonable for a delicious meal.

It's fun to experiment by substituting other meat varieties for beef.

How to Judge Doneness of Meats

Most people are picky about how they want their meat cooked. A couple factors that must be used when cooking meat are the thickness of cut, the weight of the pan, and degree of heat used.

The guidelines below are for steaks at room temperature, about 2–inches thick, cooked over medium-heat.

Rare: Brown outer crust, deep-red interior and juicy. Cook 3 to 4 minutes per side.

Medium-Rare: Brown outer crust, pink inside, with a red center. Cook 5 to 6 minutes per side.

Medium-Well: Brown outer crust, with a pink center. Cook 7 to 8 minutes per side.

Well-Done: Brown outer crust, completely cooked and grey throughout. Cook 9 to 10 minutes per side.

Broiled Flank Steak with a Wangy Tangy Sauce

Easy recipe to prepare and cook. Will become a favorite when you're in a hurry.

1	pound beef flank steak
2	tablespoons vegetable oil
2	parsley sprigs for garnish

Wangy Tangy Sauce

1	tablespoon salted butter
¼	cup tomato ketchup
1	tablespoon dry prepared mustard
½	teaspoon Worcestershire sauce
⅛	teaspoon onion salt

Preparing Wangy Tangy Sauce: Melt butter in saucepan and add remaining ingredients. Heat and stir. Do not boil and do not reheat, as this causes sauce to curdle.

Broil lightly oiled flank steak 3 to 4 minutes per side on charcoal grill or in broiler in oven. Slice diagonally, against the grain, very thin and place on plates. Cover with Wangy Tangy Sauce, garnish with parsley sprigs and serve.

Yield: 2 servings

Beef Tenderloin with Wild Mushroom Sauce

In this recipe, you will take a filet and cut it in half to form medallions.

2	6–ounce beef loin tenderloin steaks cut in half lengthwise, use tall cuts
¼	cup all-purpose flour
1	pinch salt and white pepper to taste
2	tablespoons vegetable oil
1	order Red Skin Ranch Herb Smashed Potatoes, *see page 185*
2	parsley sprigs for garnish

Wild Mushroom Sauce

1	tablespoon salted butter
1	tablespoon shallots, minced
3	ounces shiitakie mushrooms, washed
½	cup dry red wine
¼	cup heavy whipping cream
1	cup Brown Sauce, *see page 200*
½	tablespoon parsley, chopped

Cut filets in half to form four pieces of beef. Season flour with salt and white pepper; dredge meat in flour. In large sauté pan over moderate heat add oil and beef and sauté until meat is almost at desired temperature remove from skillet.

Preparing Wild Mushroom Sauce: In sauté pan add butter, garlic, and mushrooms. Cook until shallots start to brown. Add red wine; bring to a simmer and reduce in half. Add heavy cream; reduce until cream starts to thicken. Add brown sauce; bring to a boil. Return beef and parsley to sauté pan and simmer 1 minute more.

Place Red Skin Ranch Herb Smashed Potatoes in middle of large platter. Arrange beef around potatoes and spoon mushrooms and sauce over top. Garnish with parsley sprigs and serve family style.

Yield: 2 servings

Herb-Garlic Marinated Chuck Steak

Marinating chuck steak will add an abundance of flavor.

1	pound beef chuck shoulder steak, boneless

Herb-Garlic Marinade

¼	medium onion, chopped
½	tablespoon parsley, chopped
½	tablespoon white vinegar
¼	cup vegetable oil
2	teaspoons Dijon mustard
1	tablespoon garlic, minced
¼	teaspoon thyme leaves, crushed

1	order Red Skin Ranch Herb Smashed Potatoes, *see page 185*
1	cup Brown Sauce, *see page 200*
2	parsley sprigs for garnish

Preparing Herb-Garlic Marinade: In a medium size mixing bowl combine chopped onion, parsley, vinegar, oil, mustard, garlic, and thyme. Blend thoroughly.

Place beef chuck shoulder steak in medium broiler pan. Cover with Herb-Garlic Marinade, spreading evenly on both sides. Cover and marinate in refrigerator for 6 to 8 hours, turning at least once.

Preheat broiler to high heat. Place steak on rack in broiler pan so surface is about 5–inches from heat source. Broil on each side, until desired doneness. To serve steak, slice diagonally across the grain into thin slices. Place Red Skin Ranch Herb Smashed Potatoes in small soup cup and turn upside down on one side of plate to shape potatoes. In front of potatoes, fan out chuck steak slices. Serve with brown sauce and garnish with parsley sprigs.

Yield: 2 servings

Filet Mignon Wrapped with Pastry Dough

You can substitute a store-bought soft pie shell for homemade in this recipe.

2	tablespoon vegetable oil
1	12 ounce beef loin tenderloin steak
1	pinch salt and white pepper
¼	cup liver pate, canned or from deli

1	large egg, white only
1	cup Brown Sauce, *see page 200*

Pastry Dough

¾	cup all-purpose flour
¼	cup shortening
1	large egg yolk, beaten
1½	tablespoons cold water

Heat oil in sauté pan over moderate high heat. Season filet with salt and white pepper and sauté for 2 minutes on both sides. The more well done you like your meat the more you will cook it at this stage. Remove from pan. Refrigerate about 10 minutes on cool surface.

Preparing Pastry Dough: For pastry dough, combine flour and small pinch of salt. Cut in shortening until pieces are the size of small peas. Combine egg yolk and water. Add to flour mixture, tossing with a fork until moistened. (If necessary add small amount of water.) On floured surface, roll out dough into 11 x 7 inch rectangle.

Spread pastry with liver pate to within 1–inch of edges. Center meat atop pastry. Wrap pastry around meat, overlapping long sides. Brush edges with beaten egg white and seal. Trim excess pastry from ends; fold up and brush edges of ends with egg white and seal. Lift up filet wrapped with dough and place seam side down in a greased shallow baking pan. Roll trimmings to make cutouts. Brush with egg white over pastry. Bake in a 400°F oven about 25 minutes or once pastry is golden color yet dough is cooked. Serve with brown sauce. Garnish plate as desired.

Yield: 2 servings

Mom's Meatloaf Surprise with Mushrooms

Meatloaf surprise is just adding a twist to your mom's meatloaf. For a real surprise try Turkey Meatloaf *on page 133.*

½	3 ounces canned sliced mushrooms
¼	cup milk
1	large egg
¼	cup chili sauce
½	teaspoon Worcestershire sauce
¼	teaspoon salt
¼	teaspoon thyme leaves dried
½	cup dry bread crumbs

1	pound beef chuck, ground
1	hardboiled egg, cut into 4 wedges
½	tablespoon Parmesan cheese, grated
½	tablespoon parsley, chopped
¼	cup tomato ketchup
2	sprigs parsley for garnish

Preheat oven to 375°F drain mushrooms well, reserving liquid; and set aside. Combine liquid with milk to make a ½ cup of liquid. In a large mixing bowl, beat egg with a fork. Stir in milk mixture, chili sauce, Worcestershire, salt, thyme, and bread crumbs. With a fork lightly mix until bread crumbs are thoroughly moistened. Add ground beef chuck; mix just until well combined, using hands if necessary.

Place half the meat mixture in a medium size baking dish and, using moistened hands, form into a rectangular shape.

Arrange egg wedges and mushroom slices over mixture; sprinkle with cheese and parsley. Top with remaining meat mixture. Shape into a loaf; cover with ¼ cup of tomato ketchup and bake 45 minutes or until meat loaf is cooked. Remove and place on a platter,garnish with parsley sprigs. Serve meatloaf family style with your favorite accompaniments.

Yield: 2 servings

Onion-Bacon Cheeseburger Deluxe

Ground beef is clearly the most commonly used meat of them all.

4	strips smoked bacon, cooked
1	medium onion, chopped
1	pound beef chuck, ground
1	teaspoon Worcestershire sauce
1	pinch salt and white pepper
3	sesame seed Kaiser rolls
3	slices sharp cheddar cheese
	large sliced kosher dill pickles
2	lettuce leaves, washed
¼	cup mayonnaise
1	vine ripe tomato, sliced

In a large sauté pan over moderate heat oil and add beef. Sauté until meat is almost at desired doneness and remove from skillet. Sauté bacon strips and onions in skillet until bacon is cooked. Drain and place the bacon and onion to the side for later.

Place beef chuck in a large mixing bowl. Add Worcestershire sauce, salt, and white pepper. Blend ingredients thoroughly. Shape mixture into 2 plump, round, slightly flattened patties. Heat sauté pan over moderate heat. Cook hamburger 6 to 10 minutes or until desired doneness. Before removing cover burgers with grilled onions and top with cheddar cheese place cover on top 1 minute to melt cheese. Cut rolls in half crosswise; place under broiler or on grill until cut side of roll is lightly browned.

Spread mayonnaise on roll; arrange lettuce leaves on bottom of rolls. Top each roll with sliced pickles, hamburger, bacon strips, and tomato slices. Add your favorite condiments and serve.

Yield: 2 servings

Power Marinated Beef Kabobs over Saffron Rice

When making beef kabobs always use a tender cut of meat. You can use either wooden or metal skewers 10 to 12 inches long.

12	ounces beef loin tenderloin steak, cut into twelve 1-inch cubes
4	large skewers
4	medium mushrooms
1	red bell pepper, cut into 8 squares
½	medium onion, cut into one inch chunks
1	order Saffron Rice, *see page 189*

Power Marinade

¾	cup olive oil
3	tablespoons red wine vinegar
2	tablespoons Dijon mustard
2	tablespoons garlic, minced
⅛	teaspoon salt
⅛	teaspoon white pepper, ground

Preparing Power Marinade: In a large mixing bowl combine oil, vinegar, mustard, garlic, salt, and white pepper. Mix thoroughly.

Combine beef and vegetables in large bowl. Marinate 4 to 6 hours in refrigerator.

Make Saffron Rice, following recipe *on page 189*. Set aside and keep warm.

Remove beef and vegetables from marinade, and bring marinade to a boil. Alternately thread beef and vegetables onto 4 skewers. Grill or broil kabobs, while turning and basting with marinade, 6 to 10 minutes or to desired doneness. Serve the kabobs over Saffron Rice, dribble with extra hot marinade. Garnish as desired.

Yield: 2 servings

Sautéed Sirloin Burger with a Red Wine Sauce

And you thought you were tired of burgers... wait till you try this one!

1	pound beef sirloin, ground
¼	cup all-purpose flour
1	teaspoon vegetable oil
1	pinch salt and white pepper to taste
2	parsley sprigs for garnish

Red Wine Sauce

1	tablespoon salted butter
1	teaspoon shallots, minced
6	mushrooms, sliced
½	cup dry red wine
1	cup Brown Sauce, *see page 200*

Form ground sirloin into two oblong even shapes. Season flour with salt and pepper; dredge meat. In a large sauté pan over moderate heat add oil and beef and sauté until meat is almost at desired doneness. Remove burger from skillet; drain grease and return sauté pan to stove.

Preparing Red Wine Sauce: In sauté pan, add butter, shallots, and mushrooms. Cook until shallots start to lightly brown; add red wine. Bring to a simmer and reduce in half. Add brown sauce and bring to a boil. Return beef and parsley to sauté pan and simmer for 2 to 3 minutes or until hot.

Arrange sirloin burgers on a platter; spoon mushrooms and sauce over top. Garnish with parsley sprigs.

Yield: 2 servings

Super-Duper Meatball Stroganoff

This recipe uses meatballs rather than traditional beef tips.

Meatballs

1	pound beef chuck, ground
¼	pinch salt
⅛	pinch white pepper
¼	teaspoon dried dill weed
½	tablespoon A-1 steak sauce
1	cup dry bread crumbs
½	large egg
1	tablespoon vegetable oil
8	ounces fettuccine pasta, *see page 102*

Super-Duper Sour Cream Sauce

1	tablespoon salted butter
1	onion, chopped fine
6	large mushrooms, washed and sliced
2	tablespoons all-purpose flour
1	teaspoon tomato ketchup
1	cup Beef Stock, *see page 203*
¼	cup sour cream

Preparing Super-Duper Meatballs: In a large mixing bowl, lightly toss chuck with salt, white pepper, dill, A-1 sauce, bread crumbs, and egg; mix until well combined. Gently shape this mixture into ten super meatballs.

Sauté meatballs in oil until well browned all over. Reduce heat and simmer 8 minutes, constantly stirring. Remove meatballs.

Preparing Sour Cream Sauce: In medium size pan sauté over moderate heat; add butter, onions, and mushrooms. Sauté for 3 minutes. Remove from heat, add flour and stir to a smooth paste. Cook for 1 minute. Add beef bouillon and ketchup. Bing to a boil, stirring constantly. Add meat balls. Simmer gently 5 minutes, or until heated through.

Stir in sour cream; cook, stirring and over low heat, 3 minutes, or until sauce is hot. Serve over top of fettuccine pasta. Garnish as desired.

Yield: 2 servings

Stuffed Yellow and Red Bell Peppers with Tomato Basil Sauce

The red and yellow bell peppers are sweet and make a colorful dish.

2	cups Tomato Basil Sauce, *see page 201*
2	medium yellow bell peppers
2	medium red bell peppers
½	tablespoon olive oil
½	pound beef round, ground
¼	onion, diced
½	teaspoon Worcestershire sauce
½	tablespoon olive oil
2	cups Seasoned Rice, *see page 188*
2	basil leaves for garnish

Prepare Tomato Basil sauce, following recipe *on page 201.*

Slice tops from the peppers and remove seeds. Season inside peppers with salt and pepper. Set peppers and tops to the side.

In a large sauté pan over moderate heat cook ground beef, onion, and Worcestershire until meat is no longer pink; drain off excess grease. Stir in a ½ cup of tomato basil sauce and ½ cup of seasoned cooked rice, mix thoroughly.

Fill peppers with meat and rice mixture; replace tops. Place, in a shallow baking dish with some water. Bake in 375°F oven 40 to 50 minutes, or until peppers are tender. Place peppers on top a bed of leftover hot seasoned rice, dribble with tomato basil sauce. Garnish plate with basil leaves. Serve family style with excess tomato basil on the side.

Yield: 2 servings

Veal Strips with Tricolor Bell Peppers

Red, yellow, and green peppers are very colorful and flavorful to serve.

½	pound veal leg cutlets
1	tablespoon oil
½	medium green bell pepper, thinly sliced
½	medium yellow bell pepper, thinly sliced
½	medium red bell pepper, thinly sliced

½	medium onion, thinly sliced
¼	teaspoon salt
1	tablespoon garlic, minced
¼	cup green onions, chopped
½	teaspoon granulated sugar
1	dash of white pepper
2	tablespoons sherry
¼	teaspoon ginger powder
⅓	cup beef stock, *see page 203*
1	tablespoon corn starch
2	tablespoon soy sauce
1	order Seasoned Rice, *see page 188*

To make veal easier to slice, place in freezer for 20 minutes. Slice into ¼–inch slivers. Warm oil in sauté pan over moderate heat. When hot, add peppers, onion, salt, garlic, and green onions. Cook, stirring constantly, over high heat, about 3 minutes.

Add veal slivers and cook, another 2 minutes, while stirring a few times. Add sugar, white pepper, sherry, and ginger; cook, stirring, about 1 minute.

Add beef stock and bring to a simmer. In a small bowl blend corn starch with soy sauce and ¼ cup of water. Add mixture to sauté pan, stirring until sauce is thickened and translucent. Serve over a bed of Seasoned Rice.

Yield: 2 servings

Veal Patarica with Fontina Cheese and Vermouth

Fontina cheese has a mild, nutty flavor, melts easily and smoothly and is very creamy.

4	3-ounce veal leg cutlets, boneless
1	pinch salt and white pepper
¼	cup all-purpose flour
1	tablespoon olive oil
1	tablespoon salted butter
1	tablespoon shallots, minced
½	cup dry vermouth
1	cup Brown Sauce, *see page 200*
1	tablespoon lemon juice

6	asparagus spears, cooked
4	slices fontina cheese
2	parsley sprigs for garnish

Place veal between two plastic sheets and using mallet flatten to ⅛-inch thickness. *(See Flattening Chicken Breast Tips on page 118).* Season cutlets with salt and white pepper, and dredge with flour.

Heat oil in a large sauté pan over moderate heat. Add veal cutlets; sauté for 2 minutes on each side or until browned. Remove veal from sauté pan and set to the side.

Drain oil from sauté pan, add butter, and heat until foamy. Add shallots, vermouth, and lemon juice. Simmer until reduced in half. Add brown sauce and simmer. Remove ¾ of the sauce and place to the side. Arrange veal in sauté pan, so pieces overlap each other and place 3 asparagus spears on top. Smother with Fontina cheese. Cover sauté pan and cook 1 to 2 minutes or until cheese is melted. Carefully remove with spatula and place on two plates. Dribble excess sauce around veal. Garnish with parsley sprigs.

Yield: 2 servings

Veal and Eggplant with a Creamy Vodka Sauce

In this recipe the veal is sauteed with flour while the eggplant is coated with a Francaise mix. The combination will become a favorite.

4	3 ounce veal leg cutlets
1	pinch salt and white pepper to taste
½	cup all-purpose flour
½	cup sun-dried tomatoes, julienne strips
2	tablespoons olive oil
1	large egg
1	tablespoon Parmesan cheese
½	tablespoon parsley, chopped
¼	medium eggplant, peeled and sliced thin
1	tablespoon salted butter
1	tablespoon shallots, minced
¼	cup vodka
½	cup heavy cream
½	cup Brown Sauce, *see page 200*

¼   cup Tomato Basil Sauce, *see page 201*
¼   cup fresh chopped basil
2   thin slices prosciutto
4   slices mozzarella cheese
2   parsley sprigs for garnish

Place veal between two plastic sheets and using mallet flatten to ⅛–inch thickness. *(See Flattening Chicken Breast Tips on page 118).* Season cutlets with salt and white pepper, and dredge with flour.

Prepare sun-dried tomatoes for use; follow the directions on their package (if dry, soak in hot water 30 minutes before cutting). Cut into julienne strips.

Heat oil in large sauté pan over moderate-high heat. Add veal and cook for 2 minutes on each side, or until browned. Remove to warming dish.

Preparing Francaise Mix: Break eggs into mixing bowl and whip. Add Parmesan cheese and parsley. Whisk thoroughly.

Flour eggplant and dip in Francaise mix, coating thoroughly on all sides. Place eggplant in sauté pan and cook on both sides until egg starts to lightly brown, and eggplant is cooked. Remove eggplant and place to the side.

Drain oil from sauté pan, add butter, and heat until foamy. Add shallots and cook 30 seconds. Remove the pan at least 2 feet from the burner and pour vodka, from a jigger, into the pan.

Carefully replace the pan on the burner. Hold a long-handled match over pan and the vodka will ignite automatically. Once the flames go out, add heavy cream and sun-dried-tomatoes simmer until the mixture starts to thicken. Add brown sauce, tomato basil sauce and basil, and bring to a simmer for 4 to 5 minutes. Remove ¾ of the sauce from the pan and place to the side.

Arrange cutlets in the skillet so each pair are overlapping slightly. Place prosciutto on top, cover with eggplant, and then top with slices of fresh mozzarella. Cover pan and cook 1 to 2 minutes, or until cheese is melted.

Carefully remove portions with spatula and place on top of serving platter. Dribble veal and eggplant with sauce, but don't cover cheese. Garnish with parsley sprigs.

Yield: 2 servings

Frenched Veal Chops with Oyster Mushrooms

Frenched chops are rib chops that have had the meat and fat trimmed away from both sides of the bone. A great job for the butcher. Oyster mushrooms are large whitish-gray mushrooms, with an elegant appearance.

3	tablespoons vegetable oil
2	12-ounce veal loin rib chops
1	pinch salt and white pepper to taste
2	tablespoons shallots, minced
4	ounces oyster mushrooms
2	tablespoons brandy`
½	cup heavy whipping cream
½	cup Brown Sauce, *see page 200*
2	tablespoons basil, chopped
2	parsley sprigs for garnish

Heat 2 tablespoons of oil in a large sauté pan over moderate heat. Season veal chops with salt and white pepper. Add chops and cook 4 to 6 minutes on each side, or until cooked thoroughly; remove from sauté pan, and keep warm.

Drain oil from sauté pan, add butter, and heat until foamy. Add shallots and mushrooms, and cook until mushrooms are soft, about 4 minutes. Remove the pan at least 2 feet from the burner and pour brandy, from a jigger, into the pan.

Carefully replace the pan on the burner, Hold a long-handled match over pan and the brandy will ignite automatically. Once the flames go out, add cream slowly and heat until sauce is slightly thickened. Add brown sauce and basil, simmer 2 minutes. Place veal chops on plates; spoon sauce and mushrooms on top. Garnish with parsley sprigs.

Yield: 2 servings

Veal with Apples and Tarragon

Cutlets are cut from the leg and are available thinly sliced.

1	large granny green apple
4	3 ounce veal leg cutlets, pounded out
1	pinch salt and white pepper to taste
¼	cup all-purpose flour
3	tablespoons olive oil
¼	cup dry white wine

½	cup heavy whipping cream
¼	cup Brown Sauce, *see page 200*
1	tablespoon tarragon, chopped
2	tarragon leaves for garnish

Peel apple and cut in half. Remove core and slice in bite size pieces.

Place veal between two plastic sheets and using mallet flatten to ⅛-inch thickness. *(See Flattening Chicken Breast Tips on page 118).* Season cutlets with salt and white pepper, and dredge with flour.

Heat 2 tablespoons of oil in a large sauté pan over moderate heat. Add veal and cook for 2 minutes on each side, or until well browned. Remove to warming dish. Heat oil in sauté pan, add apples and cook until slightly brown. Add wine to sauté pan and bring to a boil. Next, add cream slowly, cook until sauce is slightly thickened. Add Brown Sauce and season to taste with salt and white pepper. Stir in chopped tarragon. Return veal to skillet and simmer 2 minutes. Place two cutlets on each plate; top with sauce and apples. Garnish with tarragon leaves.

Yield: 2 servings

Braised Pork Chops with Apple-Raisin Stuffing

Pork chops are cut from the loin and can be stuffed, broiled, pan fried or braised. Serve with apple sauce.

Apple-Raisin Stuffing

¼	cup celery, diced
1	tablespoon onion, fine chopped
2	tablespoons salted butter or margarine, melted
½	cup day old bread cubes
⅓	cup apple, peeled and diced
1	pinch salt and white pepper to taste
⅛	teaspoon ground sage

2	1- inch thick pork loin rib chops, with pockets
2	cups apple juice, sweetened
1	cup Brown Sauce, *see page 200*
2	parsley sprigs for garnish

Preparing Apple-Raisin Stuffing: Melt butter in sauté pan over moderate heat. Add the celery and onion. Cook vegetables until tender, about 6 to 7 minutes. Remove from heat. Add bread crumbs, apple, salt, white pepper, and sage. Mix well with a large fork.

Pat chops dry with paper towels. Fill pockets of chops with apple raisin stuffing mixture.

Preheat oven to 325°F. In a large sauté pan over moderate heat, slowly brown pork chops well on both sides, about 12 minutes in all.

Remove chops to casserole dish. Sprinkle with salt and white pepper, and pour in apple juice.

Bake, covered 30 minutes, and uncovered 30 minutes (about 1 hour in all), or until chops are tender. Remove chops and scrape juice and drippings into small saucepan. Add brown sauce and bring to simmer. Serve with brown sauce spooned over top. Garnish with parsley sprigs and serve.

Yield: 2 servings

Pork Tenderloin with Honey, Sesame, and Cilantro

Served with rice and vegetables, this dish will quickly become a favorite of yours.

1	boneless pork loin roast, 2 to 3 pounds
½	cup beef stock, *see page 203*
1	tablespoon cornstarch
2	tablespoons water cold
2	orange slices for garnish
2	parsley sprigs for garnish

Honey, Sesame, and Cilantro Marinade

¼	cup honey
¼	cup sesame oil
¼	cup soy sauce
½	cup pineapple juice
¼	cup cilantro, chopped
1	tablespoon garlic, minced
1	teaspoon ginger powder

Preparing Honey, Sesame, and Cilantro Marinade: Mix ingredients listed for

Honey, Sesame, and Cilantro Marinade in a large bowl. Add pork loin, refrigerate and marinate over night, turning over at least once.

Preheat oven to 325°F. Brown marinated pork loin on all sides in large sauté pan over moderate-high heat. Remove browned meat to a heavy ovenproof pan and add remaining marinade. Cover pan and cook in oven for about 1 hour or until internal temperature of meat registers at 170°F, using a meat thermometer.

Remove meat from pan to serving platter and keep warm. Strain cooking liquid and skim off fat. Place liquid and beef stock in small saucepan and bring to boil. Mix cornstarch and 2 tablespoon cold water into a paste. (If you use too much cornstarch, your sauce will be too thick, so add just a little at time until you reach the desired consistency.) Using a wire whisk slowly whip cornstarch mixture into pan. Heat sauce slowly until it thickens. Serve pork loin family style garnished with orange slices and parsley sprigs, with sauce on the side.

Yield: 2 servings

Belgium Endive and Ham Au Gratin

Endive will need to be simmered in beef bouillon to add flavor. Select a specialty ham such as smoked.

4	large heads Belgium endive
1	cup beef stock, *see page 203*
8	slices cooked ham
½	cup dry bread crumbs
1	cup Mornay Sauce, *see page 199*
2	tablespoons butter or margarine, melted
1	cup Tomato Basil Sauce, *see page 201*
2	parsley sprigs for garnish

In a medium size saucepan over moderate heat, simmer endive in beef stock about 20 minutes and drain beef stock and save. Slice endive in half lengthwise. Roll each half in a slice of ham. Use a toothpick to hold meat if needed. Arrange in ungreased baking dish. Mix half of bread crumbs in Mornay sauce. Smother ham and endive with the sauce. Sprinkle excess bread crumbs on top and dribble with melted butter. Add beef stock to baking dish.

Bake at 350°F for 20 minutes. Place 4 ham rolls on each plate in a half fan shape. Dribble with tomato sauce. Serve excess sauces on the side. Garnish with parsley sprigs.

Yield: 2 serving

Ham Rolls with Cranberry Glaze

Stuffed and glazed with cranberry. You will think it's Thanksgiving every day!

Cranberry Glaze

½	cup jellied cranberry sauce
2	tablespoons dark corn syrup
1	tablespoon red wine vinegar
¼	cup beef stock, *see page 203*
⅛	teaspoon allspice

Bread Stuffing

3	tablespoons salted butter
⅓	cup celery, diced
¼	medium onion, diced
⅓	teaspoon garlic, minced
2	cups bread crumbs
¼	teaspoon Worcestershire sauce
1	pinch salt and white pepper to taste

4	large slices cooked ham, ¼–inch thick
2	parsley sprigs for garnish

Preparing Cranberry Glaze: In a small saucepan, combine cranberry sauce, corn syrup, vinegar, beef stock, and allspice. Cook over low heat, stirring constantly, until sauce is melted and mixture is smooth.

Preparing Bread Stuffing: In sauté pan over moderate heat place butter, celery, onion, and garlic. Cook until onion is transparent about 5 minutes. Remove from heat and add bread crumbs, Worcestershire sauce, salt, and white pepper. Mix thoroughly. If stuffing is a little dry add a few tablespoons of beef stock used in cranberry glaze.

Place ham on flat surface, arrange ¼ of stuffing mix on each ham slice, and roll "jelly roll" style. Secure with wooden picks. In sauté pan over moderate heat, add butter and ham rolls. Cook on one side 2 minutes, turn over and add cranberry glaze; cover and cook an additional 10 minutes. Place ham rolls on plates, smother with cranberry glaze and serve. Garnish with parsley sprigs.

Yield: 2 servings

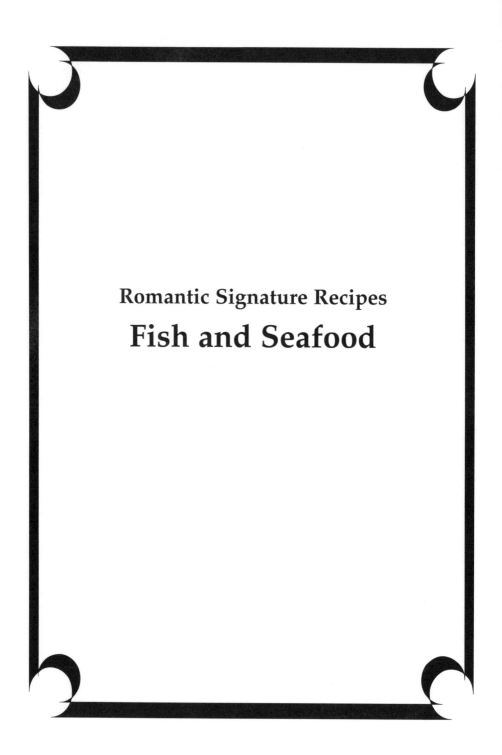

Romantic Signature Recipes

Fish and Seafood

The Swimming Part of a Relationship

Have you ever felt like you are swimming upstream? You keep trying but you don't go anywhere. When nothing will work, learn to swim with the current and your relationships and life will become easier to work within.

Talk and Listen

Talking is sharing but listening is caring and sharing. So practice talking and most important listening, and in the end you will always be sharing and caring.

Acts of Perpetual Emotions

Yell – Noise with no logic
Whisper – Soothing
Threats – Will be resisted all the way
Understanding – Willing
Ignore – Eye for an eye
Friends – I care for you
Force – Will never change a opinion
Demonstrate – I like that

Selecting Fish and Seafood

The lakes, rivers, and oceans of the world are full of hundreds of species of delicious seafood. Today, seafood is shipped from all over the world but is extremely perishable and should be treated accordingly.

Fresh seafood, when available, is always the best way to go, and can sometimes be purchased right at the pier.

Frozen seafood is your second choice, with the best selection usually available at local specialty fish markets.

Deciding whether fresh or frozen seafood is used is entirely up to you. In any event, seafood should not smell too fishy. This is a sure sign of age or improper handling by the fishmonger or store.

Calamari (Squid): Has a firm, chewy texture and mildly sweet flavor.

Clams: Clams have an edible flesh inside of two hinged shells. Atlantic clams range in size from little necks to cherrystones to large chowder clams, and also include small soft shell steamers. Scrub clam shells well before eating.

Conch: Conch flesh is tough, but may be tenderized by long, slow cooking, or by pounding with a mallet. Conch should have a sweet flavor, never too fishy!

Crabs: These crustaceans are imported from both the Atlantic and Pacific Ocean, as well the Gulf of Mexico. Dungeness and blue crab have edible meat in the body and claw. In the Alaskan king crab and spider crab the edible meat is in the legs and claws. When shopping, always choose crabmeat that will fit your needs and the way you intend to serve it.

Lobster: There are two types of lobster available: spiny lobster contains edible meat in the tail only; Maine lobster has edible meat in the tail as well as both claws. Lobster shells turn a bright red when cooked.

Frequently referred to as the "king of the shellfish," the northern lobster is classed among the most highly prized of all shellfish.

Frozen spiny lobster tails have several species of spiny lobster, weighing from 4 ounces to more than a pound each, are sold on the market.

Mussels: Have a smooth, bluish–black shell with a deep yellow or orange flesh.

Mussels should only be purchased live or precooked. Avoid any which are open and check for a sweet smell. Scrub mussels with a brush to remove the "beard" on the shells before cooking.

Oysters: When purchasing oysters they should be either alive, pre-shucked, in jars, or smoked (packed in tins). Live oysters should have their shells tightly closed. A great aphrodisiac, so they say.

Scallops: Sea scallops are about ½ to 1–inch thick. Bay scallops are much smaller.

Shrimp: Shrimp come in brown, white, and pink varieties. Both cooked and raw shrimp should feel firm and smell sweet. Removal of the black intestinal vein (deveining) should be done on all shrimp before you eat them.

Flat Fish vs. Round Fish: Fish are generally classified into two categories – round fish and flat fish. Round fish can either be cooked whole, or cut off the bone, into either steaks, or two fillets; examples are salmon, dolphin, and snapper. Flat fish such as sole and flounder are cut into filets.

Crabmeat Hint

When preparing crabmeat, be sure to pick out and discard any pieces of shell or cartilage with a fork.

Lemon Crowns

Lemons are irreplaceable as a garnish for seafood. The flavor adds zest and the color is pleasing. Available year round. When buying look for bright yellow and firm but not too hard.

How to Cut Lemon Crowns: Using a paring knife cut the lemon with deep zigzags, around side of lemon.

Cut off base of lemon so it will sit up straight.

Cutting Scallion Flowers

Scallions are white onions that are harvested while they are young. Scallions are primarily used as a very edible garnish, despite their strong flavor.

How to Cut Scallion Flowers: Choose scallions with well developed bulbs for preparing flowers. To prepare scallion flowers start by cutting 3-inch lengths. Using a paring knife make many slits into the thick end, thin slivers. Allow the flower to open in ice water. Use for garnishing seafood.

Only cut halfway through.

How to Clean Shrimp

Removal of the black intestine (deveining) should be done to all shrimp before you eat them.

Using a small, sharp knife, make a shallow cut along the back side of the shrimp. To remove shells from shrimp, use your fingers to peel towards the side. (Leaving the very end of the tail on sometimes makes things easier.) Lift shell up and over and peel around to other side. Discard shells. Remove the small, black intestine that runs along the back with knife. Wash under cold water as you devein shrimp.

How to Split Whole Lobsters

Splitting lobsters is no big deal–split 'em at the belly, and crack 'em on the back.

How to split lobsters: Place your lobster on a cutting board, belly side up. Using a French chef's knife, thrust into the head and bring the knife down through the center line of the lobster to split it in half. (Be careful not to split the lobster all the way through the back side!) Using a clean towel, crack the back of the shell, spreading the lobster open. Remove the stomach and vein. The tomalley in the lobster can be added to the stuffing if you like. (However, many people think it's "Gross"! — If you do use it, don't tell anyone!) Crack the claws, using a French chef's knife or nut cracker (if using a Maine lobster).

How to Eat a Lobster

When serving northern lobster, a bib is recommended for wearing while cracking claws. In fine restaurants a small bowl of hot water and wet towel or bev naps are used for cleaning hands after touching lobster shell.

1. When eating a lobster served in the shell, use small lobster or cocktail fork to remove the meat from the tail.

2. With regular knife and fork, cut the lobster meat and dip each fork full into melted butter.

3. Use a lobster cracker or nutcracker to break the shell of the big claws. Tasty chunks of solid meat are inside.

4. Pull off each little claw and suck out the sweet tasty morsel of meat.

5. Final search uncovers tidbits in the shell–good to the last bite.

Broiled Seafood à la Boca

Seafood prepared in garlic herb butter always has a great taste.

10	large sea scallops, with side muscles removed
4	large shrimp, peeled and deveined
2	3-ounce fish fillets
6	mussels, washed and debeard
½	cup dry bread crumbs
1	teaspoon paprika
¼	tablespoon lemon juice
2	lemon crowns for garnish, *see page 159*
2	parsley sprigs for garnish

Garlic–Herb Butter

6	tablespoons butter or margarine
1	tablespoon garlic, minced
¼	cup dry white wine
1	tablespoon Dijon mustard
¼	teaspoon oregano, chopped
¼	teaspoon basil, chopped
¼	teaspoon tarragon, chopped
½	lemon, squeezed for juice
1	teaspoon Worcestershire sauce
1	pinch of salt and white pepper to taste

Arrange seafood in two small ovenproof glass baking dishes. Place to the side.

Preparing Garlic Herb Butter: Melt butter in a small sauté pan over moderate heat. When butter is melted remove from heat and add remaining ingredients listed for Garlic-Herb Butter. Blend thoroughly.

Pour garlic herb butter over top of seafood. Sprinkle with bread crumbs, which will soak up extra liquid and add flavor. Next, sprinkle on paprika, and you're ready to bake.

Bake seafood in preheated oven, at 350°F for 10 to 12 minutes, or until seafood is done. Remove from oven and serve in baking dishes on two plates. Garnish and serve.

Yield: 2 servings

Orange Roughy with a Mango-Pepper Relish

Mango-Pepper Relish can be used for chicken as well as fish.

Mango-Pepper Relish

1	large ripe mango, diced
¼	cup green bell pepper, diced
¼	cup olive oil
½	medium lime, squeezed for juice
3	tablespoons rice vinegar
2	tablespoons basil, chopped
1	pinch salt and white pepper to taste

2	8–ounce orange roughy fillets, boned and skinned
¼	cup salted butter, melted
1	teaspoon paprika
¼	cup dry white wine
1	lemon, squeezed for juice
1	tablespoon lemon juice
2	lemon crowns for garnish, *see page 159*
2	parsley sprigs for garnish

Preparing Mango-Pepper Relish: In mixing bowl place ingredients listed for Mango-Pepper Relish, toss thoroughly.

In shallow baking pan, grease bottom and place orange roughy fillets. Brush top with melted butter then sprinkle paprika on top in an even coat. Next add melted butter, white wine and lemon juice to pan this will give fish flavor while cooking.

In preheated oven at 325°F bake fish until a light golden brown color or until fish is done, about 8 to 12 minutes. Remove from oven and place fish on two plates. Serve with Mango-Pepper Relish. Garnish with lemon crowns and parsley sprigs.

Yield: 2 servings

Poached Salmon with Cucumber Dill Salsa

The vegetables will add a nice flavor to fish when poached. Cucumber is light and refreshing and rice vinegar is light tasting.

Cucumber Dill Salsa

2	large cucumbers
1	tablespoon dill, chopped
¼	cup corn oil
¼	cup rice vinegar
1	pinch salt and white pepper to taste

2	7-ounce salmon fillets, skinned and boned
½	medium carrot, diced
¼	medium onion, sliced
½	medium leek, chopped
¼	medium garlic clove
5	small parsley sprigs
1	lemon, cut in half
4	whole black peppercorns
2	lemon crowns for garnish, *see page 159*
2	parsley sprigs for garnish

Preparing Cucumber Dill Salsa: Peel cucumbers and cut in half lengthwise. Using a spoon, scoop out seeds and pulp. Dice cucumbers. In a small mixing bowl add cucumber, dill, olive oil, and vinegar. Mix thoroughly. Adjust flavor with salt and white pepper, place to the side. Let salsa sit 2 hours to allow flavors to blend.

How to Poach Fish: To poach fish, pour about 4 cups (or as needed to cover fish) of water in a saucepan big enough to hold fish. Add carrot, onion, leek, garlic, parsley, lemon, peppercorns, and salt. Slowly bring this mixture to a boil, over medium heat. Simmer 10 minutes, reduce heat, and lower salmon gently into stock. Poach salmon in stock for about 10 to 12 minutes, or until fish flakes easily when tested with fork and done inside.

Carefully remove fish from poaching liquid when done, place on plate and cover half of fish with cucumber salsa. Garnish with lemon crowns and parsley sprigs.

Yield: 2 servings

Red Snapper Francaise with Lemon Caper Sauce

These little pickled buds called capers are from the Mediterranean and are very tasty.

Francaise Mix

2	large eggs
1	tablespoons Parmesan cheese
1	tablespoon parsley, chopped

½	cup Beurre Blanc, *see page 197*
2	8-ounce red snapper filets, boneless and skinless
½	cup all-purpose flour
1	tablespoon lemon juice
2	lemon crowns for garnish, *see page 159*
2	parsley sprigs for garnish

Preparing Francaise Mix: Crack eggs into a large mixing bowl and whip. Add Parmesan cheese and parsley, and whisk thoroughly to make Francaise mix.

Following recipe on *page 197* prepare Beurre Blanc and set to the side until needed.

Warm oil in a large sauté pan, over moderate heat. Coat snapper with flour on all sides, then dip snapper in Francaise mix, coat on all sides. Place snappers in the sauté pan and cook for 5 minutes on each side, or just until lightly golden brown. Remove snapper and place on baking sheet and place in 300°F until fish is cooked if necessary.

Place fillets on plates and pour sauce over top. Garnish with lemon crowns and parsley sprigs.

Yield: 2 servings

Salmon with Leeks and Sherry en Papillote

In this recipe, you'll steam your fish in a paper bag, which seals in the flavors.

2	7-ounce salmon fillets, boneless and skinless
2	ounces salted butter
1	cup leeks, julienne *see page 114*
½	medium red pepper, julienne

¼	medium red onion, julienne
4	mushrooms, sliced
2	tablespoons dry sherry
½	medium lemon, squeezed for juice
2	large pieces parchment paper 10 x 17 inches
½	cup vegetable oil
1	pinch salt and white pepper to taste
1	tablespoon lemon juice
2	lemon crowns for garnish, *see page 159*
2	parsley sprigs for garnish

In small sauté pan over moderate high heat, combine butter, leeks, peppers, onion, and mushrooms. Cook for 2 minutes. Add sherry and lemon juice, simmer for 30 seconds. Remove from heat and adjust flavor with salt and white pepper.

Bag Cutting and Folding: Cut large heart shapes out of baking parchment paper. This is done by folding paper in half and cutting out half a heart from the folded side (aluminum foil may be used in place of parchment). The heart must be big enough to hold the fish and vegetables, and still have room for crimping the edges. Oil both sides of parchment hearts.

Place fish on one side of the heart. Cover with sautéed vegetables and dribble with liquid. Fold over the other half of the heart. Starting at the top of heart, fold and crimp the open edges every one inch, as shown on next page. As you make a new crimp, hold the previous one in place. When you reach the bottom of the heart, fold the point under to hold it in place. The En Papillote is now ready to bake.

Place in preheated 350°F oven, bake until the parchment is puffed and lightly browned, about 15 to 20 minutes. Remove from oven, unwrap, and place fillets on plates. Garnish and serve immediately (*When opening parchment, be especially careful of escaping steam*).

Yield: 2 servings

Cancun Coconut Shrimp with a Peachy Dipping Sauce and Fried Plantains

Coconut shrimp are a favorite of mine …Try 'em, you'll like 'em, too!

10	large shrimp, peeled and deveined
½	cup coconut, shredded
¼	cup unsalted peanuts

½	cup all-purpose flour
1	large egg
½	tablespoon soy sauce
1	quart oil for deep frying
1	small green plantain
2	lemon crowns for garnish, *see page 159*
2	scallion flowers for garnish, *see page 159*
2	parsley sprigs for garnish

Peachy Dipping Sauce

1	8-ounce can sliced peaches, drained
2	tablespoons brown sugar
2	tablespoons tomato ketchup
1	tablespoon rice vinegar
1	tablespoon soy sauce
2	teaspoons cornstarch

Place coconut and peanuts in food processor. Process using an on and off pulsing action until peanuts are ground.

Toss shrimp in flour until well coated. In small mixing bowl combine egg, soy sauce. Add shrimp to egg mixture; toss until coated. Lightly coat with coconut-peanut mixture. Refrigerate until ready to cook.

Preparing Peachy Dipping Sauce: Combine ingredients for dipping sauce in a food processor. Process until peaches are chopped. Place mixture in a saucepan and bring to simmer over moderate heat. Boil 1 minute, or until thickened, stirring constantly. Pour into a small serving bowl and set aside. Sauce can be served warm or cold.

Heat oil in a heavy 2-quart saucepan over medium heat until deep fat thermometer registers 350°F. Fry shrimp a few pieces at a time, 4 to 5 minutes or until golden brown. Adjust heat to allow temperature to return to 350°F between each batch. Place on paper towels to drain grease.

Peel plantains, and cut lengthwise into thin slices. Place in deep fryer and cook about 3 to 5 minutes per piece. Fan out shrimp and dribble sauce over the top. Place fried plantains between shrimp. Garnish with lemon crowns, scallion flowers, and parsley sprigs.

Yield: 2 servings

Newlywed Stuffed Shrimp

In this recipe you will butterfly large shrimp, top with a fantastic crabmeat mixture, and bake to perfection. Very impressive and easy to prepare!

10	large shrimp, peel, devein, and butterfly, with tails left on
¼	cup dry white wine
⅛	cup salted butter melted
¼	teaspoon paprika
1	cup Saffron Rice, *see page 189*
2	lemon crowns for garnish, *see page 159*
2	parsley sprigs for garnish

Crabmeat Stuffing

4	ounces crabmeat
4	tablespoons unsalted butter
1	tablespoon garlic, minced
¼	cup onion, chopped fine
¼	cup celery, chopped fine
¼	cup white wine
1	teaspoon Worcestershire sauce
⅛	teaspoon Tabasco® sauce
1	large egg
4	cups fluffy white bread crumbs

Preparing Crabmeat Stuffing: In a large sauté pan over moderate heat melt butter. Add garlic, onion, and celery. Cook for 10 minutes, or until celery is tender. Add white wine, Worcestershire, and Tabasco®. Simmer for 3 to 4 minutes. Place mixture in medium mixing bowl and add crabmeat, egg, and bread crumbs. Mix thoroughly. Let mix cool, then form 10 equal balls out of the crabmeat stuffing mix.

Place butterfly shrimp in baking pan, split side down. Press balls of stuffing on each shrimp, and gently squeeze in place. Turn tail towards stuffing. Sprinkle with paprika, and add white wine, butter, and water to pan. In preheated oven, bake at 325°F for about 8 to 10 minutes or until stuffing is hot throughout and has a light brown color.

Remove from oven and serve on bed of saffron rice divided between two plates. Garnish with lemon crowns and parsley sprigs.

Yield: 2 servings

Boiled Northern Lobsters

In this recipe you will boil whole lobsters, split, serve or use meat for recipes in the back. When serving see How to Eat a Lobster *on page 160.*

2	live northern lobster (1 pound each)
3	quarts boiling water
3	tablespoons salt
¼	cup melted butter
2	lemon crowns for garnish, *see page 159*
2	parsley sprigs for garnish

Plunge lobsters head first into boiling salted water. Cover and return to boiling point. Simmer for 20 minutes. Drain. Place lobster on its back. With a sharp knife cut in half lengthwise. Remove the stomach, which is just back of the head, and intestinal vein, which runs from the stomach to the tip of the tail. Do not discard the green liver and coral roe; they are delicious. Crack claws. Serve with butter and garnish with lemon crowns and parsley sprigs.

Yield: 2 servings

Broiled Boiled Lobsters

In this recipe you will boil a live lobster then broil before serving.

2	boiled cooked lobsters, *see recipe above*
1	tablespoon salted butter or margarine, melted
1	pinch salt
1	pinch white pepper
1	pinch paprika
¼	cup butter or margarine, melted
1	tablespoon lemon juice
2	lemon crowns for garnish, *see page 159*
2	parsley sprigs for garnish

Lay lobsters open as flat as possible on a broiler pan. Brush lobster meat with butter. Sprinkle with pepper and paprika. Broil about 4–inches from source of heat for 5 minutes or until lightly browned. Combine butter and lemon juice, garnish and serve with lobster. Garnish with lemon crowns and parsley sprigs.

Yield: 2 servings

Broiled Spiny Lobster Tails

Serve with corn on the cob and melted butter.

2	frozen spiny lobsters tails (5 to 8 ounces each)
⅓	cup butter or margarine, melted
½	teaspoon salt
1	pinch white pepper
1	pinch paprika
¾	cup butter or margarine, melted
3	tablespoons lemon juice
2	lemon crowns for garnish, *see page 159*
2	parsley sprigs for garnish

Thaw lobster tails. Cut in half lengthwise. Lay lobster tails open as flat as possible on a broiler pan. Brush lobster meat with butter. Sprinkle with salt, pepper, and paprika. Broil about 4–inches form source of heat for 10 to 15 minutes, depending on size of lobster tails. Combine butter and lemon juice; serve with lobster tails. Garnish with lemon crowns and parsley sprigs.

Yield: 2 servings

Old Fashioned Baked Stuffed Lobsters

Now a secret of the restaurants are revealed in this recipe.

2	live northern lobsters (1 pound each)
2	cups soft bread cubes
1	tablespoon butter or margarine melted
1	tablespoon onion grated
1	pinch garlic salt
1	cup clarified butter, *see page 193*
2	lemon crowns for garnish, *see page 159*
2	parsley sprigs for garnish

Place lobster on its back; insert a sharp knife between body shell and tail segment, cutting down to sever the spinal cord. Cut in half lengthwise. Remove the stomach, which is just back of the head, and the intestinal vein, which runs from the stomach to the tip of the tail. Remove and save the green liver and coral roe. Crack claws.

Combine bread cubes, butter, onion, garlic salt, green liver, and coral roe. Place in body cavity and spread over surface of tail meat. Place on baking pan, 15½ x 10½ x 1–inch. Bake in hot oven, 400°F for 20 to 25 minutes or until lightly browned. Remove from oven and serve immediately. Serve with a small cup of clarified butter. Garnish with lemon crowns and parsley sprigs.

Yield: 2 servings

Whole Stuffed Lobster Feast with Ritz Crackers

Simple and easy to prepare, nothing looks as impressive as a whole broiled lobster stuffed.

2	live northern lobsters, 1 to 1½ pounders, split and cleaned
½	cup clarified butter, *see page 193*
2	lemon crowns for garnish, *see page 159*
2	parsley sprigs for garnish

Ritz Cracker Stuffing

3	ounces unsalted butter
3	cups crushed Ritz® crackers
2	tablespoons parsley, chopped

Preparing Ritz® Cracker Stuffing: Combine melted butter, Ritz® crackers, and chopped parsley. Fold together.

For instructions on how to split lobsters, *see page 160* . On a baking sheet, place split lobsters upside down and stuff the body cavity with Ritz® cracker mix *(Do not cover the tail meat).* Place a weight or small ovenproof bowl on end of tails so it will not curl up while baking. Brush tails with melted butter.

Place lobsters in preheated 400°F for 15 to 20 minutes, or until done. Remove from oven and serve immediately. Serve with a small cup of clarified butter. Garnish with lemon crowns and parsley sprigs.

Yield: 2 servings

Cheddar Baked Stuffed Lobsters

In this recipe you will make baked stuffed lobsters but will add your favorite cheese for extra flavor.

2	live northern lobsters (1 pound each)
1½	cups soft bread cubes
1	tablespoon butter or margarine melted

½	cup cheddar cheese grated
1	pinch paprika
1	tablespoon lemon juice
2	lemon crowns for garnish, *see page 159*
2	parsley sprigs for garnish

Place lobster on its back; insert a sharp knife between body shell and tail segment, cutting down to sever the spinal cord. Cut in half lengthwise. Remove the stomach, which is just back of the head, and the intestinal vein, which in runs from the stomach to the tip of the tail. Remove and save the green liver and coral roe. Crack claws.

Combine bread cubes, butter, cheese, green liver, and coral roe. Place in body cavity and spread over surface of tail meat. Place on a large baking pan. Bake in hot oven, 400°F, for 20 to 25 minutes or until lobster meat is cooked. Remove from oven and serve immediately. Serve with a small cup of clarified butter. Garnish with lemon crowns and parsley sprigs.

Yield: 2 servings

Lobster Thermidor

A classical recipe that when served in the shells of the lobster will look great and taste fantastic.

2	live Maine northern lobsters (1 pound each)
2	tablespoon butter or margarine,
2	tablespoon all purpose flour
½	teaspoon salt
1½	teaspoon powdered mustard
1	dash cayenne pepper
1	pint coffee cream
1	can (4 ounces) mushroom stems and pieces, drained
¼	cup Parmesan cheese
¼	teaspoon paprika
1	tablespoon lemon juice
2	lemon crowns for garnish, *see page 159*
2	parsley sprigs for garnish

Split lobster lengthwise and remove meat *(page 160)*. Clean shells and rinse. Cut lobster meat into ½-inch pieces. Melt butter; blend in flour and seasonings. Add cream gradually and cook until thick and smooth, stirring constantly. Add mushroom and lobster meat. Place in shells. Sprinkle with cheese and paprika. Place on a cookie sheet, 15½ x 12 inches.

Bake in a hot oven, 400°F, for 10 minutes or until brown. Remove from oven and serve immediately. Serve with a small cup of clarified butter. Garnish with lemon crowns and parsley sprigs.

Yield: 2 servings

Homemade Passionate Crabcakes

Lump crabmeat is the best crabmeat to use.

Homemade Passionate Crabcakes

2	cups fluffy white bread crumbs
4	ounces jumbo lump crabmeat, checked for shells
¼	cup celery, diced fine
2	tablespoons onion, diced fine
¼	tablespoon all-purpose flour
1	teaspoon Old Bay® seasoning
⅛	teaspoon Tabasco® sauce
⅛	teaspoon ginger powder
1	large egg
2	tablespoons mayonnaise

1/2	cup oil, for frying
½	cup Mustard Sauce, *see page 194*
½	cup Cocktail Sauce, *see page 194*
/2	cup Tarter Sauce with Capers, *see page 194*
2	lemon crowns for garnish, *see page 159*
2	parsley sprigs for garnish

Preparing Homemade Passionate Crab Cakes: Mix bread in food processor to produce a fluffy bread crumb mix. In mixing bowl, add bread crumbs, crab-meat, celery, onion, flour, Old Bay®, Tabasco®, ginger, egg, and mayonnaise. Mix thoroughly. Portion crab mix into four even piles to form crab cakes. Mix should have a moldable consistency. You may have to add more bread or liquid as needed.

In a large sauté pan, over moderate heat, add enough oil to coat bottom of pan. Sauté crab cakes on both sides until golden brown. When done, place crab cakes on paper towels to drain grease. Serve immediately with mustard and cocktail sauce. Garnish plates with lemon crowns and parsley sprigs.

Yield: 2 servings

Sautéed Scallops with Mushrooms and Green Onions

Scallops will be served in a tasty sherry sauce.

1	cup Béchamel Sauce, *see page 199*
1	pound large sea scallops
2	tablespoons butter or margarine
1	tablespoon garlic, minced
¼	pound mushrooms, thinly sliced
¼	cup green onion, chopped
¼	small red pepper, chopped
¼	teaspoon salt
¼	cup dry sherry
½	lemon, squeezed for juice
1	dash white pepper
1	dash of cayenne
2	scallion flowers for garnish, *see page 159*
2	lemon crowns for garnish, *see page 159*
2	parsley sprigs for garnish
8	ounces pasta, cooked and well drained

Following recipe *on page 199*, make béchamel sauce (use heavy cream).

Wash scallops in cold water; drain.

Place scallops in large sauté pan over moderate heat. Add water to cover scallops and bring to a boil. Reduce heat and simmer, uncovered, 2 to 3 minutes, or until scallops are tender. Drain, and set aside.

In the same skillet, melt butter. Sauté garlic, mushrooms, green onions, and red pepper for 5 minutes, stirring occasionally. Add sherry and lemon juice cook 1 minute additional.

Next add béchamel sauce, salt, white pepper, and cayenne. Bring to a boil, stirring constantly. Remove from heat, add scallops and reheat gently. Serve hot over pasta. Garnish with scallion flowers, lemon crowns and parsley sprigs then serve.

Yield: 2 servings

White Clam Sauce with Roasted Garlic over Linguine

Roasted garlic will add a nice tasty appeal. To make a red clam sauce just add tomato basil toward the end.

1	tablespoon olive oil
2	cloves garlic, peeled and bulbs left whole
1	can (6½ ounces) chopped clams, undrained
1	tablespoon parsley, chopped
¼	cup dry white wine
1	teaspoon basil, chopped
2	drops Tabasco® sauce
1	pinch white pepper
8	ounces Linguine, cooked and well drained
2	lemon crowns for garnish, *see page 159*
2	parsley sprigs for garnish

Mince 4 bulbs or 1 tablespoon of garlic and set to the side. In medium sauté pan over moderate heat add olive oil and garlic bulbs. Cook until garlic is lightly brown and soft. *(Or follow Garlic Roasting Techniques on 114).* Remove bulbs from sauté pan and place to the side.

Drain clams, reserving liquid. In pan with olive oil, add garlic, and minced parsley. Sauté until garlic sizzles and its aroma is in the air. Add wine and reduce in half. Add reserved clam liquid to sauté pan. Reduce heat to low. Simmer 3 minutes, stirring occasionally. Add clams, basil, Tabasco®, and pepper. Simmer 5 minutes, stirring occasionally. Place hot linguine in large soup bowls and add clam sauce. Toss lightly to coat, and garnish with roasted garlic, lemon crowns and parsley sprigs.

Yield: 2 servings

Pan Fried Buttermilk Oysters

The oysters are soaked in buttermilk, breaded with cornmeal, and fried until golden brown. When deep frying, use a fresh oil to ensure quality. Peanut oil is one of my favorites.

14	large oysters shucked
½	cup buttermilk
¼	cup all-purpose flour
1	large egg, mixed with 1 teaspoon water
¼	tablespoon parsley chopped
1	pinch salt and white pepper to taste
1	cup oil, for deep frying
½	cup Cocktail Sauce, *see page 194*
1	order Cole Slaw
2	lemon crowns for garnish, *see page 159*
2	parsley sprigs for garnish

Shuck oysters, and soak in buttermilk for 3 to 4 hours to enhance flavor. Next coat oysters in flour and egg wash. Combine cornmeal, parsley, salt and pepper. Place oysters in mix and coat evenly.

Heat oil in sauté pan over moderate heat. When oil is hot, fry oysters on both sides about 2 minutes or until golden brown. Remove and place oysters on paper towel to drain grease. Place oysters on 2 plates and serve with cocktail sauce and your favorite coleslaw. Garnish with lemon crowns and parsley sprigs.

Yield: 2 servings

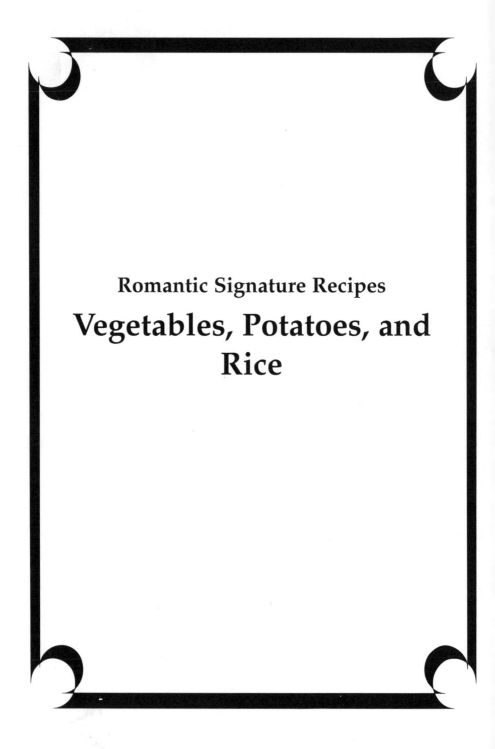

Romantic Signature Recipes

Vegetables, Potatoes, and Rice

The Growing and Health Part of a Relationship

When mom said eat your vegetables, starches, and grains to grow stronger she wasn't joking. In your relationship, eat properly, exercise, and surround yourself with positive mental attitude people, and you will grow stronger in all your relationships.

(PMA.) Positive Mental Attitude

You owe it to yourself to grow mentally and physically so you will be the best that you can be.

Power Growth Ideas

Read books on positive mental attitude

Learn to set a side a time to center (meditate)

Workout together

Vegetable Tips

You should give as much attention to preparing your vegetables as you do to preparing meat. A well seasoned vegetable is both a pleasure to eat, and very nutritious.

Modern methods of preparation and shipping make almost every vegetable available at your market, at any season. There is no excuse for monotony in your vegetable diet.

The most important rule about cooking vegetables is to avoid over cooking. Properly cooked vegetables should have a bit of crunch to them and should never be served limp or soggy.

Retaining Nutritional Value: Cook vegetables for as short as time as possible. Steaming vegetables will help to avoid any great loss of nutrients. Baking vegetables in their skin will prevent loss of water-soluble nutrients. Potatoes and winter squash are prepared this way.

Retaining Natural Colors: A short cooking time is of great advantage here. Cooking processes reduce the chlorophyll content of green vegetables. For white and red vegetables, a small amount of vinegar or lemon juice added to the water will help in preventing color changes.

Obtaining Excellent flavors: The freshness of vegetables will have a lot to do with their flavor when cooked. As vegetables lose their freshness some of their sugar turns to starch, and they lose some sweetness. Some of the flavor compounds of vegetables will escape during cooking.

Keeping Pleasing Textures: Vegetables should have desirable texture (slightly crisp) and should not be mushy when cooked. As always, opinions will vary in respect to what is considered desirable texture for cooked vegetables.

Steaming vegetables has the advantage of keeping their color bright and eliminating the need to discard liquid that is filled with nutrients.

Vegetable Seasoning Hints

Vegetables usually need some seasoning to make them more appealing. The quickest and easiest seasoning is a little butter, salt, and white pepper. The flavor of many vegetables may be further enhanced by adding a few drops of fresh lemon juice, simple cream sauces, or more elegant such as Hollandaise sauce. Toppings for vegetables include nuts, cheese, herbs, or bread crumbs.

Cutting Vegetables with Mandolin

Use a mandolin to cut vegetables if you can find one. A mandolin is a compact, hand-operated machine with various adjustable blades for thin to thick slicing and for Julienne and French-Fry Cutting. Julienne, *see page 114.*

Mandolins come in both wood and stainless steel frame models with folding legs. Great for cutting firm vegetables and potatoes with uniformity and precision.

Asparagus Bundles

Place two bundles as vegetable on plates when creating entrées.

¼	pound fresh asparagus
1	large carrot, peeled
¼	cup olive oil
1	tablespoon dried tarragon leaves
1	pinch salt and white pepper to taste

To prepare asparagus, cut off tough end of spears so they are 3 to 4 inches long. (Peeling stems with a vegetable peeler is optional.)

Rinse asparagus, and place in steamer basket. Place steamer basket in large saucepan; add 1–inch water. Cover, and bring to a boil over moderately-high heat; steam asparagus about 5 minutes, or until crisp and tender. Remove and set to the side.

Using a peeler, make long thin slices down side of carrot until you have 4 long (about 4 to 5 inches) thin slices. Steam or parboil carrots until slightly tender and they curl up.

To make asparagus bundles, divide into 4 even piles. Wrap each pile with a carrot slice to create a bundle. Place bundles in steamer. Cover. Bring to a boil over high heat. Steam for 3 to 4 minutes, or until asparagus is hot.

In a small sauté pan over moderate heat, add olive oil and tarragon, cook 30 seconds. Place bundles on warm serving plates and top with garlic mixture. Season with salt and white pepper, and serve.

Yield: 2 servings

Cheese Buttered Dill Parsnips

Parsnips are creamy-white roots that have a sweet flavor.

1	pound parsnips
2	ounces butter or margarine
½	cup sharp cheddar cheese, grated
¼	cup brown sugar
1	pinch salt and white pepper
1	tablespoon dill, chopped
1	boiling water as needed

Wash parsnips and cut lengthwise into quarters. Cut each quarter into 3-inch pieces. Place in medium saucepan. Add boiling water to measure 1–inch and simmer, covered, for 20 minutes, or just until tender.

Remove parsnips and drain, if necessary (most of the liquid will have evaporated). Cool slightly, and remove cores from parsnips.

Melt butter in the same saucepan, using moderate heat. Stir in cheese, brown sugar, salt, and pepper.

Add parsnip, stirring gently, over low heat, until cheese is melted and parsnips are well coated. Stir in dill, and serve at once.

Yield: 2 servings

Honey Cinnamon Acorn Squash

Honey cinnamon and brown sugar make acorn squash tasting like candy.

2	acorn squash, cut in half, with seeds removed
3	tablespoons butter, melted
¼	cup brown sugar
⅛	teaspoon cinnamon, ground
1	pinch salt and white pepper
¼	cup honey

Preheat oven to 350°F.

Scrub squash. Cut in half, lengthwise. Remove seeds and stringy fibers.

Arrange squash, cut side down, in shallow baking pan. Surround with ½–inch hot water. Bake for 30 minutes. In a small mixing bowl combine butter, brown sugar, cinnamon, salt, pepper, and honey. Pour off excess liquid from baking pan; turn squash cut side up.

Pour honey-cinnamon over squash and bake additional 15 to 20 minutes, basting now and then with honey and cinnamon that has gathered in cup of squash. Using a fork, check to see if squash is tender and ready to serve.

Yield: 2 servings

Cauliflower Florets with Fu Fu Crumbs

Fu Fu crumbs add a nice flavor to cauliflower.

Fu Fu Crumbs

½	cup dry bread crumbs
2	ounces butter, melted
½	teaspoon parsley, chopped
1	pinch salt and white pepper to taste

1	medium head cauliflower
2	ounces butter, melted

Preparing Fu Fu Crumbs: In small mixing bowl, blend bread crumbs, butter, paprika, and parsley. Adjust flavor with salt and white pepper and mix thoroughly. (If using fresh bread, place in oven at 225°F for 20 minutes to dry. Put in food processor and purée to crumbs.)

Pick off cauliflower leaves and cut head in half. Cut off stem and break florets into big bite size pieces. In a large pot of boiling water, add salt and cook 7 to 8 minutes, or until tender but crisp. Do not over cook. Drain.

In a large sauté pan over moderate heat, melt ¼ cup butter. Add cauliflower and Fu Fu crumbs. Toss cauliflower until coated and serve.

Yield: 2 servings

Green Beans Vinaigrette

Experiment with different dressings until you find just the right combination.

¼	pound green beans, with ends removed
1	tablespoon vegetable oil
1	medium red bell pepper, sliced thin
¼	medium onion, chopped
1	pinch salt and white pepper
½	cup Vinaigrette Dressing with Capers and Herbs, *see page 197*

In a pan of boiling water cook beans for 4 to 8 minutes until tender but crisp, and drain. Add oil to sauté pan over moderate heat. Add onion and red pepper, salt and white pepper, cook for 4 to 5 minutes, or until onions are transparent. Add green beans and Vinaigrette dressing. Simmer until beans are hot and ready to serve.

Yield: 2 servings

Carrot and Zucchini Ribbons

Use a mandolin to cut the vegetables, *see page 179* cutting vegetables with mandolin. If no mandolin is available, a sharp peeler will work wonders.

1	medium zucchini
1	small carrot, peeled
2	tablespoons olive oil
1	teaspoon garlic, minced
1	teaspoon red wine vinegar
1	tablespoon basil, chopped
1	pinch salt and white pepper

Cut off ends of carrot and zucchini. Using a vegetable peeler, slice carrot and zucchini from end to end to create long ribbons. (For zucchini use only outside green skin for color, save inside for tomorrow's vegetable.)

Place zucchini and carrot ribbons in steamer basket inside a large saucepan. Add 1-inch water, cover, and bring to a boil over high heat. When pan begins to steam, check vegetables for doneness. Zucchini should be crisp and tender, but not overcooked. Transfer vegetables to serving plates, using a slotted spatula.

Make sauce in a blender by adding olive oil, garlic, vinegar, basil, and salt and white pepper. Purée for 20 seconds. Dribble over top of vegetables before serving.

Yield: 2 servings

Stewed Tomatoes

Add French Dressing for extra taste.

2	large vine ripe tomatoes
¼	large bay leaf
1	ounces butter or margarine
½	tablespoon granulated sugar
1	pinch salt and white pepper
1	large pot boiling water as needed

Place tomatoes in boiling water and let stand for 1 minute. Drain; cover with cold water. Carefully peel skin. Cut tomatoes into four sections.

In small saucepan, combine tomatoes with rest of ingredients; bring to boil. Reduce heat, and simmer, covered, about 8 minutes, or until tomatoes are tender.

Yield: 2 servings

Parmesan Tomatoes with Asparagus Spears

Easy to make and makes entrée look great!

1	medium size tomatoes, cored and cut in half
⅓	cup Parmesan cheese
12	medium asparagus spears
4	red pimentos, cut into strips
1	pinch salt for cooking

Cover cut halves of tomatoes with Parmesan cheese. Bake tomato halves in oven at 350°F, or just until the Parmesan starts to melt and brown. In a saucepan, over moderate heat, bring water and salt to a simmer. Add asparagus spears and cook for 4 to 6 minutes. Remove from water and drain. Place tomatoes on one side of plate and place 3 asparagus spears on each side in a fan arrangement. Place red pimentos on asparagus. Place entrée on other side of plate and you will have a full plate presentation that is easy yet elegant.

Yield: 2 servings

Potato Pointers

You can use potatoes to create many elegant dishes. When cooking potatoes, choose a variety that is best suited for the recipe. All-purpose Idaho and russet are best for baking. Small (white, red, or new) potatoes are best for boiling and roasting.

Potatoes are very nutritious and can be fun to create as well.

Baked potatoes can be served with butter, or special toppings such as cheese, broccoli, shrimp, peppers, onions, bacon bits, etc. You get the idea.

Mashed potatoes can also be a treat when seasoned with peas, carrots, tomato or herbs. Use your imagination.

Wrapped Baked Idaho or Sweet Potatoes

Use Idaho or Russet for baking. Use your favorite toppings for baked potatoes.

2	large Idaho, russet, or sweet potatoes
2	8" x 8" sheets of tin foil
2	tablespoons butter or margarine

Prick potatoes several times with a fork or wooden skewer. Wrap potatoes tightly in foil. Bake in preheated 375°F oven about 50 to 60 minutes. Test with a fork to see if done. Unwrap and cut lengthwise to top. Squeeze potato on ends to open like a pocket. Season with, butter, and your favorite topping.

Yield: 2 servings

Garlic-Roasted Red Bliss Potatoes

An excellent way to serve red bliss potatoes.

¼	pound red bliss potatoes
½	cup corn oil
2	tablespoons garlic, minced
2	tablespoons dry bread crumbs
1	tablespoon paprika
1	pinch of salt and white pepper to taste

Preheat oven to 325°F. Scrub, wash potatoes, and cut in half. In large mixing bowl add oil, garlic, bread crumbs, paprika, salt and white pepper. Mix thoroughly. Empty potatoes into roasting pan. Bake, stirring occasionally, 40 minutes or until potatoes are tender and golden brown. Garnish with chopped fresh parsley, if desired.

Yield: 2 servings

Red Skin Ranch Herb Smashed Potatoes

Ranch dressing herb mix will have all the flavor you will need.

1	pound red bliss potatoes
1	teaspoon salt
2	ounces butter
¼	cup hot milk
¼	cup sour cream
1	tablespoon dry ranch dressing mix

Scrub potatoes thoroughly; rinse under cold running water.

Place in a large saucepan and cover with water. Add salt, bring to a boil, and reduce heat. Cover and simmer until potatoes are fork tender. Drain well; add butter, hot milk, and ranch dressing mix. Smash potatoes with a mixing motion until blended thoroughly. Return to low heat. Cook, stirring, until potatoes are heated through, adding more liquid if needed. Spoon into a warm serving dish.

Yield: 2 servings

Sweet Potato Planks with a Cinnamon Glaze

Fried wedges taste like candy yams. A real treat.

3	medium sweet potatoes
2	ounces butter
¼	cup granulated sugar
2	tablespoons cinnamon, ground
1	quart oil for deep fat frying

Peel sweet potatoes and cut lengthwise in half. Next cut each half into 3 or 4 wedges but cutting at angles inward to make planks. Precook sweet planks in a steamer or pot of boiling water until planks are fork tender yet still firm. Set to the side.

Place the oil in a heavy 2-quart saucepan over medium heat until deep fat thermometer registers 350°F. Fry sweet planks a few pieces at a time, 4 to 8 minutes, or until just golden brown. Adjust heat to allow temperature to return to 350°F between each batch. Place large sauté pan over moderate heat and get pan super-hot (Pan must be really hot to melt butter and sugar). Next add butter and sugar mix and caramelize. Add potatoes and toss in cinnamon mix. Coat sweet potatoes on all sides. Repeat again with the rest of the potatoes. Serve immediately.

Yield: 2 servings

Potato Pancakes

Potato pancakes can also be made with mashed potatoes just by adding the other ingredients.

Potato Pancakes

2	cups grated potatoes
1	teaspoon salt
2	eggs, lightly beaten
½	cup all-purpose flour
1	tablespoon lemon juice
¼	cup red onion, grated
1	tablespoon chives, chopped
½	teaspoon garlic, minced
1	pinch of salt and white pepper

3	tablespoons butter, for frying
¼	cup sour cream
¼	cup apple sauce

Preparing Potato Pancakes: Grate potatoes and toss with 1 teaspoon of salt. Place in colander and let stand for 30 minutes. Rinse potatoes and drain well. Thoroughly pat dry with kitchen towels.

In a large bowl combine grated potatoes, eggs, flour, lemon juice, red onion, chives, garlic, pinch of salt and white pepper. Mix thoroughly, and let stand for 20 minutes.

In a large sauté pan, over moderate heat, melt enough butter to coat the bottom of pan. Drop in batter with a large tablespoon and fry on both sides until browned. Place potato pancakes on paper towel to drain grease. Garnish with sour cream and apple sauce. Serve immediately.

Yield: 2 servings

Rice Review

The way in which rice is cooked depends on both the type of rice and the particular recipe.

Rice has an abundance of uses. From breakfast cereals and desserts, to a starchy replacement for potatoes.

The first rule to follow when cooking rice is to read the instructions on the packaging. Different rice requires different amounts of water, and different cooking times

How much rice to cook: Estimate about ½ cup cooked rice per serving.

• 1 cup uncooked white rice will make about 3 cups of cooked rice.

• 1 cup uncooked converted, parboiled, or brown rice will make about 4 cups of cooked rice.

• 1 cup instant precooked rice will make about 2 cups of cooked rice.

Types of Rice

Rice grows in three lengths: short, medium, and long. The difference between white and brown is in how it is milled after it has been harvested.

Some types sold in supermarkets include:

Short-Grained: Brown rice, enriched white rice, Italian rice, and precooked rice.

Long-Grained: Brown rice, enriched white rice, converted rice, precooked rice, and wild rice.

Serving Rice

The easiest way to serve rice is cook it, season it ,and spoon into a serving dish. Rice can also be served in more elegant ways.

A molded ring of rice can be served by itself, or with a filling. Rice can be also be compressed into almost any shape in a well greased container and popped onto your serving plate. Molded rice always adds a festive touch to any meal.

Seasoned Rice

Rice can be seasoned with bouillon for flavor. If you want plain rice, omit bouillon and add 1 teaspoon salt.

1	cup long grain rice
2½	cups water
½	tablespoon butter or margarine
½	bouillon chicken base cube

Measure 1 cup rice and 2½ cups water. Combine water and bouillon cube in a medium saucepan. Bring to a boil, using moderate heat.

Add rice and butter. Cover, and simmer about 20 minutes or until most of the liquid has been absorbed. Let stand for 5 minutes. Fluff with a fork, and serve.

Yield: 1¾+ cups

Confetti Rice

Rice blends well with so many ingredients that, by using your imagination, you can create many fancy side dishes. Here is one of my all-time favorites.

1	ounce butter
¼	cup red onion, chopped fine
1	tablespoon garlic, minced
½	carrot, small dice
¼	red pepper, chopped fine
½	cup zucchini outer skin, finely chopped
1	tablespoon parsley, chopped
1	cup Seasoned Rice, *see page 188*
¼	cup chicken stock or chicken consommé, *see page 203*
1	pinch white pepper

In saucepan, over moderate heat, add butter, garlic, onion, red pepper, carrot, zucchini, and chopped parsley. Cook until onions start to turn transparent and garlic aroma is in the air. Add rice, chicken stock, and white pepper. Mix thoroughly. Lower heat and simmer for 3 minutes, stirring once. Let stand 5 minutes. Fluff up with fork. Toss lightly to combine.

Yield: 2 serving

Saffron Rice

Saffron is the worlds most expensive spice. But, a little saffron goes a long way and is used both to flavor and tint food. Saffron comes in powdered form and in threads.

1	cup long grain rice
2	tablespoons butter
¼	cup onion, chopped
¼	teaspoon saffron, chopped fine
2	cups chicken consommé
1	pinch white pepper
¼	red bell pepper, chopped

In a medium saucepan over moderate heat, add butter and onions. Cook until onions start to turn transparent. Next, add chopped saffron and sauté for 20 seconds, stirring constantly. Add chicken consommé, rice, white pepper, and red bell pepper. Mix thoroughly. Lower heat and simmer for 20 minutes, stirring 3 to 4 times while rice is cooking. Remove from stove and let sit 10 minutes. Test rice for firmness and cook a little longer if needed. Serve immediately.

Yield: 2 servings

Rice and Spinach Pilaf

Spinach cooks fast, so add at the very end.

¼	cup chicken consommé
¼	onion, chopped fine
2	tablespoons butter or margarine
1½	cups Seasoned Rice cooked, *see page 188*
1	cup fresh spinach, chopped

Wash spinach and pick off stems and chop up.

In a medium saucepan over moderate heat, combine chicken consommé with onion and butter. Bring to a boil.

Add rice. Cover, and remove from heat. Let stand for 5 minutes. Fluff up with fork. Add spinach, toss lightly to combine, and serve.

Yield: 2 servings

Romantic Signature Recipes

Dressings and Sauces

The Enhancing Touches of a Relationship

Dressings will complement the fresh taste of salads and sauces are created to add flavor to the food. As every relationship will need to be smothered with sauces of loves, hugs, fun and games for that zing.

Fun and Games

Create some fun and games that you can play as the night goes on that will create excitement and fun.

Game Ideas

Strip poker or spin the bottle

Truth or dare

Karaoke song singing

Model clothes for each other

Create exotic fun.........

The Importance of Sauces

Every great cook or chef must learn how to prepare great sauces. Whether simple or more intricate, a sauce will enhance the flavor and appearance of the food it accompanies. Sauces may also add nutritional value. In this chapter, we will talk about some basic ideas and procedures for making sauces. A sauce is a thickened, flavored liquid.

All sauces fall into one of two categories: warm sauces and cold sauces. You don't have to know all of them. If you learn a few simple procedures for sauces, the rest will come easier.

Cold Sauces Varieties

Vinaigrette dressing (oil and vinegar), cocktail, cold mustard, and salsa. Cold sauce can be oil based, fruit, or vegetables and always served cold.

Warm Sauces Varieties

Hot Butter Sauce: A quick and easy way to cook meats and vegetables is in butter, seasoned with herbs, lemon juice and garlic. These are known as butter sauces. Two popular examples are garlic-herb butter and lemon butter.

Velouté (Light Stock Sauce): Is a stock-based sauce. You can use fish stock or clam juice for seafood. When thickened, is called a "roux."

Béchamel (Basic White Sauce): Is made by combining butter with flour to make a smooth paste (roux), then adding liquid (cream or milk) to the roux to form a sauce.

Tomato Sauces: These are tomato-based sauces with a combination of seasonings to add flavor, and a thickener, if needed.

Egg-Based Sauces: In an egg-based sauce, the addition of butter or oil to egg yolks causes the sauce to thicken. An example is Hollandaise sauce.

Sauce Hints

Homemade sauces will have that something extra that you will appreciate.

Thickening Agents

Thickening Agents: Roux is a thickening agent used in making sauces, soups, and gravies. Cornstarch is a thickening agent which, when mixed with water, juice, or stock and subjected to heat, provides a semi-clear glossy finish to a sauce. Sauces should be thickened just enough to coat food lightly, and yet still run off of it.

Types of Roux: The most common thickeners for savory sauces are white, blonde, or brown roux. All these are made of the same ingredients to begin with, but change in character (color) as heat is applied. To make a roux, use equal proportions by weight of fat and flour, mixed to form a thick paste. Fat can be either butter, margarine, shortening, chicken fat, oil, or rendered meat drippings.

When preparing a roux, always make sure that you completely blend in the flour, leaving no lumps. Roux should be cooked over very low heat, about 5 minutes, or longer as needed. If a roux is not cooked long enough to displace the raw taste of flour, this unpleasant flavor will overpower the strongest stocks and seasonings.

When cooking roux, mix the butter and flour thoroughly to allow the starch granules to swell evenly. If not, they later fail to absorb the liquid, and your sauces will be too thin.

Cornstarch: Cornstarch is often used when translucency is desired. When using cornstarch, smoothly blend in an adequate amount of cold liquid. Next, add the boiling liquid, stirring to prevent lumping or scorching. If you use too much, your sauce will be too thick. So, add just a little at time until you reach the desired consistency. Do not over beat a cornstarch-based sauce, as this will over-thin it.

Arrowroot: Makes a more delicately textured sauce, and is best prepared 10 minutes before use. The flavor of arrowroot is neutral and it does not need to be cooked to remove the raw flavor, as in flour. Therefore, it can be added to the sauce at a lower temperature.

Other thickeners and methods available: Egg yolks, potato starch, or reduction.

Clarified Butter

Also called "drawn butter," is great for lobster. Clarified butter has a higher smoking point, since the milk solids have been removed. Hence, it may be used to cook at a high temperature.

Preparing Clarified Butter: Using 2 pounds or more of unsalted butter, slowly melt, in a small saucepan, over low heat. Melt until separation of the milk solid, which sink to the bottom of the pan when most of the water evaporates, occurs. Skim off the foam on the surface. Next, using a large ladle, separate the clear butter from the milky residue at the bottom of the pan. This is clarified butter. You can save unused clarified butter for later use.

Yield: About 2+ cups

Cocktail Sauce

Cocktail sauce makes a great condIment for hors d'oeuvres and seafood dishes.

¼	cup tomato ketchup
¼	cup chili sauce
½	tablespoon prepared horseradish
¼	medium lemon, squeezed for juice
3	drops Tabasco® sauce
⅛	teaspoon Worcestershire sauce

Combine ingredients in a medium size mixing bowl. Whisk until well blended. Chill and serve.

Yield: ¾+ cup

Mustard Sauce

Mustard sauce is spicy, tangy, and goes great with stone crabs and crab cakes.

1	tablespoon dry white wine
⅛	teaspoon dry mustard
¼	cup mayonnaise
2	tablespoons sour cream
2	tablespoons Dijon mustard
1	tablespoon honey
¼	medium lemon, squeezed for juice

Preparing Mustard Sauce: In a small mixing bowl, add white wine and dry mustard. Blend until dissolved. Add remaining ingredients, and whisk until well blended. Chill and serve.

Yield: 1½ + cup

Tartar Sauce with Capers

Homemade tartar sauce tastes a lot better than store bought, since you can adjust the flavor to suit your taste.

½	cup mayonnaise
2	tablespoons sweet pickle relish
½	tablespoon capers

¼   medium lemon, squeezed for juice
⅛   teaspoon Worcestershire sauce
2   drops Tabasco® sauce
1   pinch salt and white pepper to taste

Preparing Tartar Sauce with Capers: Combine ingredients in a small mixing bowl. Whisk until well blended. Chill and serve.

Yield: ¾+ cup

Fantasy French Dressing

Fantasy dressing is quick to make.

½   cup salad oil
¼   cup olive oil
2   tablespoons dry white wine
¼   cup red wine vinegar
1   pinch salt and white pepper
¼   teaspoon dry mustard
2   tablespoons basil, chopped
¼   tablespoon garlic, minced

In a blender or food processor, combine all ingredients. Cover and purée 3 to 4 seconds. Refrigerate, covered, at least 2 hours. Mix well before serving.

Yield: 1¼ cups

Key West Lime Dressing

The combination of citrus fruits and mint are refreshing on a fresh salad.

½   cup salad oil
1   tablespoon cider vinegar
1½   tablespoon lime juice
2   tablespoons concentrated orange juice
1   tablespoon granulated sugar
¼   teaspoon salt
1/16   teaspoon paprika
2   tablespoons mint, chopped fresh

Combine all ingredients in blender or food processor, cover and purée 3 to 4 seconds. Refrigerate, until ready to serve. Mix well before serving.

Yield: 1¼ cups

Honey–Mustard Poppy Seed Dressing

This salad dressing is a classic one that you will love and your guests will treasure. The secret to this recipe is the oil chosen and the blending of the honey and mustard!

¼	cup honey, heat for easier blending
2	tablespoons Dijon mustard
1	cup corn oil
⅓	cup red wine vinegar
⅛	teaspoon dry mustard
½	tablespoon dry white wine
2	teaspoons poppy seeds
¼	teaspoon salt

Preparing Honey–Mustard Poppy Seed Dressing: In small mixing bowl, add hot honey and mustard, and using a wire whisk blend for 20 seconds. Next slowly blend in corn oil using a wire whisk, whip, then slowly add vinegar. Blend for 10 seconds. Blend dry mustard with white wine to form a paste. Add dry mustard and wine mix, poppy seeds, and salt. Blend for 5 seconds. Chill and serve. Whip again before serving.

Yield: 1½+ cups

Cucumber and Yogurt Dressing

Easy to make. Cayenne pepper is a hot, pungent powder made with several tropical chili peppers, so use lightly.

½	large cucumber
½	cup plain yogurt
1	pinch cayenne pepper

Peel cucumber. Halve lengthwise; remove seeds from center, and discard. Chop cucumber finely, in to ½ cup measure. Combine cucumber with rest of ingredients, mixing well. Refrigerate, until ready to serve.

Yield: 1 cup

Maple Street Dressing

Perfect for fruit salads.

½	cup maple syrup
2	tablespoons salad oil
½	tablespoon lemon juice
⅛	teaspoon paprika
⅛	teaspoon salt and celery salt
⅛	teaspoon onion powder
⅛	teaspoon dry mustard

In small mixing bowl, combine all ingredients, mix well. Cover and refrigerate until ready to serve. Mix well before serving.

Yield: ¾ cups

Vinaigrette Dressing with Capers and Herbs

Capers will have a pungent flavor that will lend a piquant taste to sauces and condiments.

1	cup salad oil
⅓	cup red wine vinegar
1	pinch salt and white pepper
2	tablespoons capers, chopped
½	tablespoon chives, chopped

In small mixing bowl, combine all ingredients and mix well. Cover, and refrigerate until ready to use. Mix before serving.

Yield: 1½ cups

Beurre Blanc

A classic French sauce, made with a shallot reduction into which cold butter is whisked in. When seasoned just right, it is excellent with seafood.

2	shallots, peeled and minced
¼	cup dry white wine
¼	cup white wine vinegar
½	pound unsalted butter, cut in ten pieces

2	teaspoon tarragon, chopped
1	teaspoon chives, chopped
¼	lemon, squeezed for juice
⅛	teaspoon Worcestershire
2	drops Tabasco sauce
1	pinch salt and white pepper to taste

Preparing Beurre Blanc: Place shallots in a heavy saucepan. Then add vinegar and wine. Bring to a simmer over moderate heat. Reduce liquid until almost completely evaporated. Lower heat and beat in butter quickly, 1 piece at a time. Beat until all butter is melted. Remove from heat, and strain into another pan so the heat will not cause the beurre blanc to break. Add remaining ingredients and adjust flavor with salt and white pepper.

Yield: 1½ cups

Hollandaise Sauce

A delicious and superb sauce for vegetables and poached fish. It's made with butter, egg yolks, and lemon juice, and seasoned for extra flavor. Hollandaise sauce is made in a double boiler to prevent eggs from turning into scrambled eggs. Also, high heat will break the sauce.

½	cup melted butter or clarified butter, *see page 193*
2	medium egg yolks
1	tablespoon lemon juice
2	drops Tabasco® sauce
2	drops Worcestershire sauce
1	pinch salt and white pepper to taste

Preparing Hollandaise Sauce: Use a double boiler, *(see page 49)* over moderate heat. Add egg yolks, a tablespoon of water and, using a wire whisk, cook egg yolks while whipping constantly, until eggs start to fluff. Remove mixing bowl from double boiler if eggs start to cook. Place back in pan and keep whipping until yolks are fluffy and will stand at peaks. Remove from heat and slowly add melted butter, whisking thoroughly until all butter is mixed in. Add remaining ingredients. Adjust flavor with salt and white pepper. Serve immediately.

Blender Method: In blender, combine egg yolks and lemon juice. Cover, and turn motor on and off once quickly. At high speed, gradually and steadily add hot butter. Add remaining ingredients and adjust flavor with salt and white pepper. Serve immediately.

Yield: 1¼ cups

Béchamel Sauce

Béchamel sauce is easy to make and great to use in other sauces while cooking. When making it, remember to use equal amounts of butter and flour. It is the amount of liquid that is added that will determine the thickness of the sauce

2	tablespoons clarified butter, *see page 193*
2	tablespoons all-purpose flour
1	cup half and half, heavy cream, or milk
1	pinch salt and white pepper to taste

Preparing Béchamel Sauce: In a small saucepan, over low-moderate heat, add butter and flour, and stir until mixture is a smooth paste. Cook for 3 to 4 minutes, stirring constantly. Next add milk very slowly, stirring constantly with a wire whisk. Cook until sauce lightly thickens. Add more liquid if too thick. Season to taste with salt and white pepper.

Yield: 1¼ cups

Mornay Sauce

A béchamel sauce to which cheese has been added–usually Parmesan and Swiss.

¼	cup Parmesan cheese, grated
¼	cup Swiss cheese, chopped
1¼	cups béchamel sauce, on the thin side

Following recipe above prepare Béchamel Sauce on the thin side.

Preparing Mornay Sauce: Add Parmesan and Swiss cheese to béchamel sauce. Cook over low heat until cheese is melted, stirring constantly. Add more liquid if needed.

Yield: 2 cups

Brown Sauce

To make brown sauce you will need a seasoned liquid to work with. Beef stock, pan drippings, beef consommé or soup, and beef broth are just a few bases you can work with.

2	tablespoons clarified butter, *see page 193*
¼	cup all-purpose flour
4	cups beef stock or broth, *see page 203*
½	tomato, chopped
½	order Mirepoix, *see page 202*

Melt butter in large sauté pan over low heat. Add flour and blend into a smooth, lump-free paste. Cook, while stirring, over low heat until mixture is lightly browned. Add the stock gradually, stirring constantly until smooth. Add the tomatoes and mirepoix, and simmer until sauce is reduced in half, stirring often. Strain through a fine sieve and serve immediately or save in refrigerator until needed.

Yield: 2 Cups+

Velouté Sauce

One of the five "mother sauces," Velouté is stock-based white sauce. Chicken, veal, or fish stock is thickened with a white roux. This sauce is used as a base for the making of other sauces

2	tablespoons clarified butter, *see page 193*
2	tablespoons all-purpose flour
1	cup stock, *see page 202*

Preparing Velouté Sauce: In a medium size sauté pan, add butter and flour to make a thick paste. Cook for 2 minutes over low heat. Let cool for a few minutes, and add stock to pan gradually, stirring constantly. Reduce and cook for 10 minutes more. Stir stock occasionally and skim top if necessary. Strain sauce and, if necessary, add more stock to thin it out. The consistency should not be too heavy. Put to side for later.

The following is a list of velouté sauces made with various stocks.

Clam Velouté: When making clam velouté sauce, use clam juice.

Chicken Velouté: When making velouté sauce use chicken stock listed *on page 203.*

Yield: 1 cup

Tomato Basil Sauce

Tomatoes are a member of the nightshade family. Vine fruits native to South America are also called tomatoes. Tomatoes have been classified as a fruit but most people think of them as vegetables.

1	tablespoon olive oil
½	tablespoon garlic, minced
¼	cup onion, chopped fine
¼	cup dry white wine
2	cups diced tomato in juice, canned
1	cup tomato purée
1	tablespoon granulated sugar
1	pinch salt and white pepper to taste
¼	cup basil, chopped

Preparing Tomato Basil Sauce: Heat olive oil in a a medium size sauce pot. Add garlic, onion, and parsley. Then sauté lightly, for a few minutes, until the garlic and onions flavor and aroma is in the air do not brown. Use lower heat in pan when cooking, so garlic and onion do not brown.

Add white wine, and reduce in half. Next add diced tomato in juice, tomato purée, and sugar. Simmer over low heat for about 30 minutes, or until sauce thickens.

In a blender, purée tomato basil sauce. Adjust seasoning with salt and white pepper. Add chopped basil and serve.

Yield: 2½ cups

Using Stocks and Bases

Stocks are very important in cooking. Basically, a stock is the strained liquid that results from the cooking of meat or fish with vegetables and other seasonings.

There is no one way to making stocks. The technique involves nothing more than filling a big pot with water and a variety of flavorful ingredients. The most important ingredient in stock are the bones–whether cooked or uncooked. If bones have a lot of meat, all the better, but lean bones will do. Cooking extracts flavors and nutrients from the vegetables and meat.

When cooking in a pinch, you can use ready-made canned products. If you use bases or products that need diluting, simmer in Mirepoix to add flavor and nutrients

Stock and Base Hints

You can buy just about any kind of ready-made stock or base in most supermarkets, if you need them in a pinch.

However, preparing your own is usually less costly, and lends more to that homemade flavor.

Mirepoix

Mirepoix is used to season sauces, soups, and stews.

2	teaspoons butter
2	teaspoons cooking oil
1	medium carrot, chopped
1	medium onion, chopped
1	stalk of celery, chopped
⅛	teaspoon dried thyme leaves
1	bay leaf, crushed
2	tablespoons sherry

Melt butter in large sauté pan over moderate heat. Add oil, carrot, onion, and celery. Sauté until soft. Add remaining ingredients, simmer until vegetables are soft.

Yield: 2+ cups

Beef Stock

Here is a simple basic stock recipe that uses beef as a base. You can substitute other varieties of meat or seafood to create a different stock.

1	order Mirepoix, *see page 202*
2	pounds beef bones
3	quarts water
¼	cup parsley stems
¼	pound beef base, as needed
1	pinch salt and white pepper to taste

Using the recipe *on page 202*, make mirepoix in a large sauce pot. When vegetables are soft, add bones, water, and parsley. Bring to a boil. (Browning of the bones in oven before adding to stock will add a dark rich color.) Reduce heat to low, and simmer for at least two hours. Skim surface until clear. Add more water while simmering, if necessary.

Remove bones and grease from stock. (Strain stock through a double thickness cheesecloth.) Discard vegetables.

Use stock to make soups, sauces, and gravies. Stocks will keep in freezer for up to 6 months and will always be available at any time to add to soups, sauces, etc.

Yield: Will vary

Chicken Stock

Try different varieties of bones from the butcher.

2	pounds chicken bones, wash thoroughly
¼	pound chicken base, as needed

Follow recipe for beef stock but substitute chicken bones and base for beef bones and base cook only 1½ hours.

Yield: 1- quart

Sunset Coulis Collection

Food Art at its finest. Use coulis to paint the entrées for a show. The Sunset Coulis collection is simple coulis that have color and are easy to make. In this section we will explore some simple coulis varieties that will create an array of tones and tastes to almost any dish.

After preparing coulis you will place coulis in squeeze bottles when ready to serve dishes pick up squeeze bottle and paint the top of plate and food for a show, color, as well as added flavor.

Art Studio Coulis Painting Ideas

The plate is the canvas and the sauces are the paint. Ladles and squeeze bottles are the brushes, so use your imagination.

Sauce painting uses contrasting colors, and placement of sauces on the plates in a fashion similar to painting. One of my favorite ways is to use a squeeze bottle to paint designs using the liquid sauce.

The coulis has to be smooth, and easy flowing consistency that is not too tight or loose

• Zigzag design

Make zigzag design by using a ketchup bottle filled with sauce and dribble sauce on side of entree on plate in a zigzag.

• Crisscross design

Make crisscross design by using a ketchup bottle filled with sauce and dribble sauce on top of entree in a crisscross design.

Hibiscus Coulis

Deep red color. Made with fresh ginger, beets, and raspberry.

½	tablespoon fresh ginger, peeled
½	cup beets, drain juice
¼	cup raspberries puree, *see page 216*

Place ingredients in food processor and purée for 1 to 2 minutes, stopping to scrape down sides twice. Using a fine strainer, strain sauce and discard pulp. If coulis is thin, reduce in saucepan over moderate heat until thickened. Place sauce in squeeze bottle and serve room temperature.

Yield: 1 cup

Mango Wasabi Coulis

Wasabi is a Japanese horseradish. Available as a paste or a powder that is blended with liquid. The combination of Dijon, mango and Wasabi pureed together is a treat.

½   cup ripe mango or mango puree
3   tablespoons Dijon mustard
1   teaspoon wasabi horseradish

Peel and remove seeds of 1 ripe mango. Place mango, Dijon, and Wasabi in a food processor. Purée for 1 to 2 minutes, stopping to scrape down sides twice. Sauce has to be puréed well. Adjust flavor with salt and white pepper. Next, using a fine strainer, strain sauce and discard pulp. If coulis is thin, reduce in small saucepan over moderate heat until thickened. Place sauce in squeeze bottle and serve at room temperature.

Yield: 2 cup

Cilantro Pesto Coulis

Pesto is an uncooked sauce made with fresh basil, garlic, pine nuts, Parmesan cheese, and olive oil. But in this recipe you, will substitute cilantro for basil. Cilantro has flavor that fits well with highly seasoned food.

¼   cup pine nuts
1   cup olive oil
¼   cup Parmesan cheese
¼   cup cilantro, chopped
1   tablespoon garlic, minced
1   pinch salt and white pepper to taste

Preparing Cilantro Pesto Coulis: In blender or food processor with metal blade, place all ingredients listed and blend thoroughly, scraping mixture down 5 to 6 times. Adjust flavor with salt and white pepper.

If coulis is too thick, thin out with a little olive oil. Place sauce in squeeze bottle and serve room temperature.

Yield: 1 cup

Sundried Tomato Coulis

California favorite, simple yet tasty and easy to make.

¼   cup gourmet tomato sauce
¼   cup sundried tomatoes

Soak sundried tomatoes in hot water for 30 minutes to soften if using dried sun-dried or read directions on sun dried package.

Place all ingredients listed for Sundried Tomato Coulis and blend thoroughly, scraping mixture down 3 to 4 times until smooth. Adjust flavor with salt and white pepper. If coulis is thick, add a drop white wine to thin.

Place sauce in squeeze bottle and serve room temperature.

Yield: 1 cup

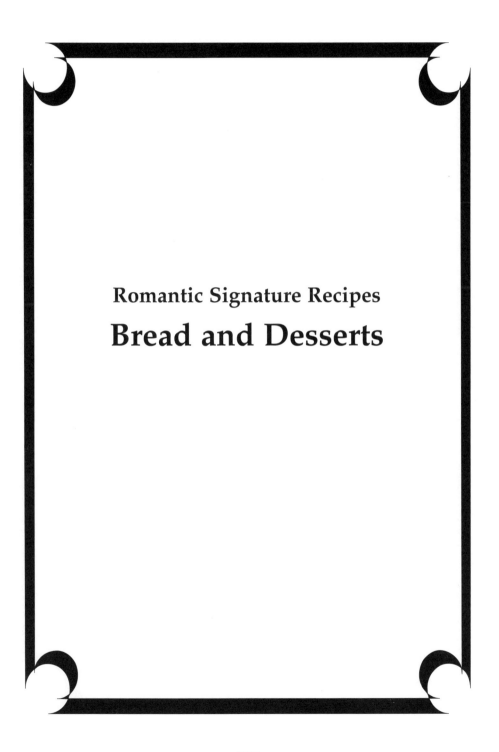

Romantic Signature Recipes

Bread and Desserts

The Climax of a Relationship

The bond of bread breaking is an old tradition that everybody should try during dinner (breaking bread to bond together). Desserts should be creative and a time to enjoy the sweet moments of the day and being together.

Creative Desserts or Desires

des•sert n. *a sweet course served at the end of a meal.*

The sweet course does not always have to be food.

Creative Ideas

Share a bottle of champagne

Feed each other chocolate-covered strawberries

Watch classic romance movies

Present a gift on a dessert plate

How to Knead

To mix or work by repeatedly folding over and pressing together, as dough, usually with the hands. Kneading smoothes dough and develops the gluten that gives it the elasticity to hold together as it expands.

Gently pick up dough from side away from you. Fold over toward you. Press out lightly with palm of hand. Give the dough a quarter turn. Repeat ten times. Gently roll out dough from center to ¾–inch thickness.

Bread Hints

Homemade bread is fun to make once in while, so the following pages contain a few of my recipes to try. Have fun, and enjoy your favorites with your partner.

Passion Curry Biscuits

Curry powder is a strong, use sparingly. Old fashioned and simple.

2	cups all-purpose flour, sifted
3	teaspoons baking powder
1	teaspoon curry powder
1	teaspoon salt
⅓	cup shortening
¾	cup milk

Preheat oven to 375°F. Sift flour into medium bowl, with baking powder, curry powder, and salt.

Cut shortening into flour mixture, with a pastry blender or two knives (used scissors fashion), until mixture resembles coarse corn meal.

Make a well in the center. Pour in ⅔ cup milk all at once. Stir quickly round the bowl, with a fork. If mixture seems too dry, add a little more milk. Make dough just moist enough (but not too wet), so it leaves the side of bowl and forms a ball. Place dough onto lightly floured board.

How to Knead: Gently grab far side of dough. Fold over toward you. Press out lightly with the palm of your hand. Give the dough a quarter turn. Repeat ten times. Gently roll out dough from the center to a ¾–inch thickness.

With floured 2½–inch biscuit cutter, cut straight down into dough, being careful not to twist cut. Place biscuits on ungreased cookie sheet. Bake 20 to 25 minutes, or until biscuits are fully cooked inside. Mix honey with butter and serve with biscuits.

Yield: 8 biscuits

Honey Pecan Whole Wheat Muffins

Everybody loves muffins. Serve warm in a basket.

1	cup all-purpose flour, sifted
2	teaspoons baking powder
½	teaspoon salt
½	cup whole wheat flour, unsifted
½	cup milk
1	large egg, well beaten
½	cup honey
¼	cup pecans, chopped fine
1	teaspoon orange peel, grated
¼	cup salad oil or melted shortening

Preheat oven to 400°F. Grease muffin tray or use 2½–inch paper muffin cups.

Sift all-purpose flour with baking powder and salt into a large bowl. Stir in whole-wheat flour, and mix well.

Combine milk with rest of ingredients in a medium bowl. Beat well with wooden spoon.

Make a well in the center of dry ingredients. Pour in the milk mixture all at once. Stir quickly with fork, until dry ingredients are just moist. Do not beat, batter should be lumpy.

Quickly dip batter into muffin-pan cups, filling not quite to two-thirds full. Bake 20 to 25 minutes, or until nicely browned and done inside. Loosen edge of each muffin with spatula; turn out. Serve hot.

Yield: 12 muffins

Homemade Bread

A versatile recipe for both bread and rolls

8	cups unbleached flour
1	tablespoon salt
3½	cups warm water
2	tablespoons honey
1	5-ounce package dry yeast

Dissolve yeast in ½ cup warm water and add rest of ingredients, reserving 2 cups flour. Beat for 1 to 2 minutes. Stir in remaining flour and mix briefly with hands. Cover and allow to rise in a warm place. When volume doubles, separate into 3 loaves and put into greased loaf pans. Let loaves continue to rise for 30 to 50 minutes.

Bake at 350° F for 10 minutes. Lower oven to 325° F and continue baking for another 35 minutes. Dough can be frozen and when thawed will rise again.

Yield: 3 loaves

Sweet Grilled Cinnamon Sticks

A sweet tooth favorite served at dinners years ago.

4	slices white bread
¼	cup margarine or butter, melted
¼	cup granulated sugar
2	teaspoons cinnamon, ground

If you have a electric griddle, use it. If not, a sauté pan will work just as well.

Trim crust from bread and cut each slice into three sticks. Brush with margarine or butter and roll in sugar combined with cinnamon.

Place on large ungreased griddle or sauté pan and grill on both sides. Turn often until golden brown on an all sides , about 2 minutes. Serve hot.

Yield: 12 sticks

Tomato, Garlic and Herb French Bread

A zesty variation of the all-time favorite.

½	loaf french bread
¼	cup olive oil
1	tablespoon garlic, minced
1	vine-ripe Tomato Concassé, *see page 114*
2	tablespoons basil, chopped
¼	cup Parmesan cheese

Slice french bread lengthwise in half. Drain juice from tomatoes. Next, in a small mixing bowl, combine olive oil, garlic, tomatoes, and basil. Mix thoroughly. Adjust flavor with salt and pepper. Smear tomato mix over flat side of french bread, spread evenly. Lay french bread on a baking sheet, flat side up sprinkle Parmesan cheese on top. Using broiler setting, toast bread, on bottom shelf of oven, until tomatoes are hot and bread is toasted around edges.

Yield: ½ loaf

Dessert the Grand Finale

Dessert should always be the perfect finale to the meal. Three senses to concentrate on when making desserts are sight, smell, and taste. Desserts can be served simply, with just a touch of decoration or it can be molded, and elegantly decorated, to form a work of art.

The Final Show

Dessert is the perfect conclusion to a meal. Think of sight, smell, and taste, when preparing your desserts. They can be served simply, with just a touch of decoration, or can be molded, and decorated into elegant works of art.

Eye appeal is always important to the presentation of food, and dessert is the last dish that your guests will see.

Dessert Garnish Suggestions: Mint sprigs, chopped nuts, whipped cream, sour cream, cream cheese, yogurt, cookies crumbs, crushed candy, shaved chocolate, etc.

In the following pages we will discuss some ways in which to add a little showtime to your dessert presentation.

Dessert Made Special with Personalize Writing, *see page 214*
Gallery of Sauces for Dessert Presentations, *see page 214 to 217*
Sugar Fruit for Garnish, *see page 218*
The Art of Romantic Feeding for Two, *see page 34 to 37*
The Art of Table-Side Cooking Desserts, *see page 70 to 74*

Using Pastry Bags

Purchase pastry bags at specialty gourmet shops. They should come supplied with an assortment of tips which you can use to create various effects.

Select the desired tip and position it securely in the pastry bags opening. Fold down the bags top, create a cuff, then fill with frosting, using a spatula or spoon. *(Do not overfill bag or contents will ooze out and be difficult to handle.)*

Unfold cuff, gather the top of the bag together and twist the top closed. Squeeze first to expel any air pockets. The bag is now ready to use.

The Art of Plate Presentation

Dessert Made Special with Personalize Writing

A showboat presentation of affection that is fun and easy to do. The art of writing words on dessert plates will add that special touch.

Words – Expression
Ideas: Marry Me •Happy Anniversary • I Love You
An art that I learned while serving slices of cake for birthdays and anniversaries at restaurants. Everybody wanted that special touch so I just added it in writing on the plate. Always use large plates or platters that have a lot of room for writing on and placing desert. Don't forget to garnish with mint leaves and dabs of whipped cream to finish the art work.

The plate is the canvas and rim of the plate is the picture frame. So create a beautiful picture that will leave a lasting impression of memories

Parchment Cones for Writing and Designing, *see page 215.*

For convenience and consistency use store bought colored *piping gel* or *little tubes of colored frosting* will work out perfect.

Gallery of Sauces for Dessert Presentations

From zigzag designs to hearts, you can have fun making designs on your desserts.

Dessert painting relies on contrasting colors, a steady hand, and very finely pointed knife or wooden toothpick.

Pour a couple tablespoons of chocolate sauce on one side of each plate, using a squeeze bottle or paper funnel. Pipe a spiral of custard sauce on top. Make designs by drawing the point of a sharp knife or wooden pick through the custard sauce and chocolate sauce.

• **Crisscross Design**

Make crisscross design by using a ketchup bottle filled with sauce and dribble sauce on top of desert and plate in a crisscross design.

• **Zigzag Design**

Make zigzag design by using a ketchup bottle filled with sauce and dribble sauce on side of desert on plate in a zigzag design.

• **Heart Design**

Make heart designs by drawing the point of a sharp knife or wooden pick through a small round circle of custard sauce that has been placed in a pool of chocolate sauce to make a heart shape design, repeat on plate.

• **Mosaic Design**

Make spider web design by drawing the point of a sharp knife or wooden pick into the middle then out at a different angle of custard sauce with spiral of Kahlúa chocolate sauce to make a mosaic design.

Parchment Cones for Writing and Designing

Parchment cones are used to decorate pastries with delicate designs of chocolate, fondue, or special piping gels.

Parchment Cones: Fold a sheet of parchment paper on the diagonal, slightly overlapping. Using a sharp knife or scissor cut out a medium size, some what shaped like a triangle (It is not necessary to form a perfect triangle using a sharp knife cut.) Place thumb and forefinger in the middle of cut diagonals to make a pivot point. Roll the parchment into a funnel shape, keeping the pivot point closed as the paper is rolled. Keep the paper taut as it is rolled. (Remember that you are forming a funnel to pipe soft liquid out of.) When the triangle has been rolled into a cone (funnel), there will be three points at the cone's top. Fold the point on the outside into the interior of the cone.

1. Parchment paper.
2. Fold slightly overlapping, cut and use bottom section.
3. Use bottom portion, roll into cone.
4. Parchment cone.

Fill the cone so it is half full. Do not overfill or it will ooze out of the top. Fold the outer points in toward the cone's center and the last corner over the top of the other points, to seal.

Cut off the tip of the cone, using a knife or scissors, to create a small opening. *(Trim a small piece at first to practice piping. Then, you can make the hole bigger if necessary.)*

Custard Sauce

Using this sauce will give texture and the perfect off-white yellowish base on which to top with a darker sauce.

2	egg yolks
½	cup heavy whipping cream
2	tablespoons powdered sugar, sifted
1	teaspoon vanilla extract

In a small heavy double boiler, combine egg yolks, heavy cream, sugar and vanilla. Whisk constantly until mixture is creamy and thick enough that the whisk leaves a visible trail on the bottom of the pan. While cooking, be careful not to let mixture overheat, or egg yolks will curdle. Remove from heat, and cool mixture, stirring occasionally. Strain for lumps.

Pour Custard Sauce on plate and spread out. Garnish with Kahlúa Chocolate Sauce or fruit purée.

Yield: 1 cup

Rose Melba Sauce

Melba is a pinkish, thickened combination of raspberries, currant jelly, and sugar.

¼	cup raspberry Melba sauce
¼	cup plain yogurt

Mix Melba and yogurt well. Strain thoroughly, and refrigerate. When ready to use, place in a plastic squeeze bottle and dribble on plates to create designs.

Yield: ½ cup

Papaya Purée or Raspberry Purée

Puréed fruit makes a nice touch. This sauce will add color and flavor to many desserts.

Papaya Purée

½	medium papaya, ripe
1	tablespoon powdered sugar, sifted

Raspberry Purée
½   pint raspberries, washed
1   tablespoon powdered sugar, sifted

Peel and deseed papaya. Wash raspberries. In a food processor, purée, scraping down sides twice while puréeing. Purée papaya and raspberry separate.

Place fruit purée in a two small saucepan over moderate heat. Add 1 to 2 tablespoons sifted powdered sugar and cook 3 to 5 minutes. If needed, add arrowroot or cornstarch to thicken. Strain fruit into a bowl through a fine strainer to remove seed and fiber, to make a smooth purée. Cool before serving.

Yield: 1+ cup

Kahlúa Chocolate Sauce

A chocolate sauce delicately flavored with a coffee liqueur made in Mexico.

1   8-ounce package semisweet chocolate morsels
1   tablespoon light corn syrup
2   tablespoons light cream
½   tablespoon boiling water or hot coffee
½   teaspoon vanilla extract
1   tablespoon Kahlúa liqueur

Melt chocolate in double boiler. Add corn syrup, stir, and slowly add cream. Stir until mixture is smooth and cook for 15 to 20 minutes. If the mixture is too thick, add coffee or water. Add extract and remove from heat. Mix Kahlúa with chocolate sauce. Place in refrigerator until ready to use. Reheat in double boiler, serve warm. When ready to use place in ketchup bottle and dribble on plates to create designs.

Yield: 1+ cup

Romance Whipped Cream

A great topping for many desserts. A favorite of mine is to always have a can of aerosol whipped cream on hand, it is easy and convenient to use.

½   cup heavy whipping cream
3   tablespoons powdered sugar
2   teaspoons vanilla extract

Using a wire whisk or electric mixer, beat heavy cream over ice cubes in a chilled mixing bowl, just until cream thickens. When peaks start to form, add sugar and vanilla. Then whip to the desired consistency.

Yield: 1¼+ cups

Sugar Fruit for Garnish

Trim your dessert presentations with sugared fruit garnish with assortment of sugared fruit.

2	small clusters of grapes
6	medium bing cherries
8	large blueberries
1	large egg white
¼	cup granulated sugar

Wash fruit. Dry with paper towels or let air-dry on towels.

In a small mixing bowl beat egg white with a fork until foamy.

Brush egg white onto each piece of fruit with pastry brush, coating all sides of fruit.

Place fruit on waxed paper that has been covered with sugar. Next sprinkle a light even coating of sugar over fruit with small spoon. If any areas of fruit are not coated repeat with egg white and sugar. Let sugared fruit stand at room temperature until coating is dry. Use as a garnish with your favorite dessert.

Yield: 2 portions

Baked Peaches ala Mode

Baked Peaches ala Mode which means served in its finest style such as with ice cream or my favorite way is just a bowl itself.

4	canned peach halves
¼	cup light-brown sugar
1	pinch cinnamon, ground
3	tablespoons cornflakes
½	tablespoon butter or margarine
2	scoops vanilla ice cream

Preheat oven to 375.

Drain peaches, reserving ¼ cup liquid. Arrange peaches cut side up, in a small baking pan. Add reserved liquid. Combine sugar and cinnamon; sprinkle evenly over peaches.

Top each peach half with 1 tablespoon of cornflakes and dot of butter; bake 15 minutes. Serve warm, spoon over a scoop of ice cream.

Yield: 2 servings

Flaming Baked Alaska

A spectacular ice cream dish covered with meringue and set on fire for show. Use blender blades to whip meringue.

3	medium scoops vanilla ice cream
1	6–inch cake layer, (any flavor)
2	large egg whites
½	teaspoon vanilla extract
¼	teaspoon cream of tartar
⅓	cup granulated sugar
2	tablespoons 151 proof Rum

Prepare cake layer about ¾–inch thick. Cut into a 4 X 4 inch squares. Allow ice cream to soften. Spoon into a small bowl lined with clear plastic. Invert ice cream over cake, and remove bowl. Shape to fit cake layer. Freeze until firm.

Making Meringue: Beat egg whites, vanilla, and cream of tartar, until egg whites are shiny. Add sugar and beat until stiff peaks form when mixing rotors are raised. Transfer cake and ice cream to a baking sheet, and remove plastic. Using a spatula, spread meringue over all of ice cream and cake, sealing edges to baking sheet. Place oven rack in the lowest position. Bake in a 500°F oven for 1 to 2 minutes or till golden brown. Place half of egg shell on top of Baked Alaska and press down until secure. Fill with 151 proof rum and take out to table. Using a long–handled match, ignite the rum. When fire subsides, discard egg shell; slice and serve.

Yield: 2 servings

Banana Bunnies

Phyllo dough or pie shell dough from the store will work wonders, if pastry dough is too much effort.

Pastry Dough

1	cup all-purpose flour
½	teaspoon salt
⅓	cup shortening

2	large bananas, green tip
2	tablespoons granulated sugar
⅓	teaspoon cinnamon, ground
½	cup strawberry yogurt
1	cup Romance Whipped Cream, *see page 217*
2	large mint leaves as garnish

Preparing Pastry Dough: Mix and sift flour and salt. Cut in 1 tablespoon of shortening with a knife. Add enough water to make a stiff dough, rolling out into an oblong piece on a slightly floured board. Next, dot with bits of shortening, using ⅓ the remaining quantity. Fold over ends to the center and fold again to make 4 layers. Press ends together and roll out. Dot again with shortening, fold and roll. Repeat this process a third time. Chill.

Peel and cut bananas in half, crosswise. Roll in sugar and cinnamon mixture. Roll out dough into two 4 x 4 inch squares of pastry about ⅛–inch thick. Place one banana on each square, and roll completely around the banana (cut edges so they don't overlap.) Bake in 350°F oven until brown and dough is cooked. Place ¼ cup yogurt in middle of each of two plates. Serve hot, on top of strawberry yogurt. Top off with romance whipped cream and mint leaves for garnish.

Yield: 2 servings

Cream Cheese Hearts with Passion Fruit Pearls

End the meal in style with this rich cheese treat!

2	6-inch cheesecloth squares
4	ounces cream cheese, softened
¼	teaspoon vanilla extract

| 2 | tablespoons powdered sugar, sifted |
| 1 | cup Romance Whipped Cream, *see page 217* |

¼	cantaloupe, peeled and deseed
½	cup raspberry purée, *see page 216*
2	large mint leaves for garnish

Line 2 one-cup heart-shaped molds (or molds of your choice) with damp cheesecloth, hanging over the edges.

In a small mixing bowl, beat cream cheese and vanilla with an electric mixer, at medium speed, until well combined. Gradually add powdered sugar, beating until fluffy. Set to the side. In another bowl, prepare romance whipped cream until soft peaks form and fold into the cream cheese mixture. Spoon into the prepared molds. Cover and chill for 6 to 24 hours.

While cheesecake molds are setting up, make your raspberry purée. With a tiny melon baller, make melon balls out of cantaloupe and place in bowl. Refrigerate until needed.

To serve, invert molds onto serving plate. While tightly holding cheesecloth ends, lift molds from cheesecloth. Carefully remove cheesecloth. Dribble raspberry purée around cream cheese heart. Surround with cantaloupe pearls, garnish with mint sprigs, and serve.

Yield: 2 servings

Melon Star Surprise

A different way to serve melon. It makes a lovely summer dessert.

2	medium cantaloupes, ripe
8	medium strawberries
½	pint raspberries
2	large pieces leaf lettuce
1	small mixture of fresh fruit that you like
2	large mint leaves for garnish

Using a very sharp knife, cut off the top of the melon in a zigzag pattern, *(see lemon crowns, on page 159)* starting about two-thirds of the way up the melon, open top. Scoop out and discard the melon seeds inside of melon. Using a melon baller scoop out balls of flesh from the inside of the lid and place in a bowl.

Wash the strawberries and raspberries, remove and discard stems. Using bottom half of melon stars fill with berries and melon balls. Place melon stars in large bowls filled with crushed ice. Garnish with mint sprig and serve.

Yield: 2 servings

Meringue Heart Sundaes

Meringue is a stiff mixture of egg white and sugar that can be formed into various shapes. In this recipe we will make heart shapes for filling with ice cream.

Meringue Hearts

3	large egg whites
⅛	teaspoon cream of tartar
¼	cup powdered sugar, sifted
¼	teaspoon vanilla extract
1	pint berries (blackberries, blueberries or raspberries)
2	scoops strawberry ice cream

With an electric mixer, beat egg white and cream of tartar until very foamy. Gradually add the sugar, a little at a time, beating well after each addition. Beat until meringue holds very stiff peaks. Add vanilla and beat 30 seconds more.

Cover baking sheet with parchment or brown baking paper. Draw two heart shapes, each 5–inches across at the widest point, on the paper. With a spatula, spread meringue over heart shapes, building up so they stand ½ in middle of heart top ¾–inch high on the edges.

Bake in preheated 275° F oven for 45 minutes. Turn oven off and let meringue shells dry in warm oven for 1½ hours.

Crush package of unsweetened, frozen strawberries. Sweeten berries and juice to taste with sugar. Place meringue hearts on plates and fill each meringue heart with a large scoop of strawberry ice cream; top with berries, and serve.

Yield: 2 servings

Minted Pineapple Boats with Creme De Menthe

You use cocktail parasols (umbrellas) to highlight this refreshing, exotic dessert.

1	small pineapple and seasonal berries as available (honeydew, cantaloupe, peaches etc.)
2	tablespoons creme de menthe
2½	cups Romance Whipped Cream, *see page 217*
2	tablespoons cashews, chopped
2	tablespoons coconut, shredded
2	pieces leaf lettuce
2	parasol umbrellas for garnish

Cut pineapple lengthwise, right through the crown of spiky leaves with a large knife, and cut out and remove the core. Cut the flesh out of the pineapple cores, while leaving their shells intact to create two boats. You will fill the two boats later.

Combine the pieces of cut pineapple with any mixture of fruit desired–melon balls, sliced peaches, pears, berries, etc. (Use enough fruit and juices to measure 2 cups). Place fruit in blender or food processor with creme de menthe, and purée. Add puréed fruit to 1½ cups romance whipped cream and fold together. Spoon the fruit mixture into the pineapple boats, and freeze until firm.

To serve, using extra whipped cream and pastry bag, pipe large rosettes of the whipped cream around the shell and sprinkle with cashews and coconut. Cover two plates with leaf lettuce, and place in pineapple boats. Garnish with cocktail parasols opened to form umbrellas, and serve.

Yield: 2 servings

Poached Peaches in Champagne

Fresh peaches poached in champagne need to be tasted to be really appreciated.

2	large ripe peaches, preferably white
2	cups dry champagne
½	cup maple syrup
½	small vanilla bean

3	large strawberries
2	tablespoons powdered sugar
¼	medium lemon, squeezed for juice
1	cup Romance Whipped Cream, *see page 217*
2	large mint leaves for garnish

Make a very light incision all around peach skins. Plunge the peaches briefly into boiling water, then into cold water, and peel. Place in a shallow pan and douse with champagne. Add the syrup and vanilla bean. Bring to a slow boil over low heat, and poach peaches at about 185°F, but do not allow to boil. If peaches are very ripe, they will be poached after 5 minutes.

Place peaches and syrup in a cool place, but do not refrigerate. Drain peaches, reserving the poaching liquid. Wash strawberries, remove any leaves, and purée in a blender or food processor. Place in a bowl and stir sugar into the purée. Stir romance whipped cream into the strawberry purée and add lemon juice.

Serve on round plates, or in glass dishes or small bowls. Line the bottom of the dishes with strawberry cream and arrange the cooled, but not chilled, peaches on top. Garnish each peach with a mint sprig. Serve the chilled poaching liquid separately in a sauce boat.

Yield: 2 servings

Romance Coated Truffles

Truffles are easy to make because of the amount of ingredients involved and not dependent upon a temperamental sugar syrup for their base.

8	ounces sweet baking chocolate, cut up
⅓	cup whipping cream
3	tablespoons butter or margarine
½	teaspoon vanilla

Romance Truffle Coatings

2	tablespoons powder sugar
2	tablespoons unsweetened cocoa powder
2	tablespoons finely chopped nuts
2	tablespoons shredded coconut

Line an 8 x 4 inch loaf dish with plastic wrap. Set aside. In a doubler boiler *(see page 49)* add chocolate, whipping cream and butter. Heat mixture until chocolate melts and mixture can be stirred smooth and shiny. Blend in vanilla or flavored extract. Pour mixture into prepared loaf dish. Refrigerate for 4 hours.

Lift chocolate mixture from dish and cut into 18 equal portions. Let stand 12 minutes.

Coat hands lightly with powdered sugar and roll each portion into balls. Work quickly when rolling mixture into balls. Chocolate mixture is rich, and melts easily. In four small bowls place coatings and roll each ball in different coatings. Place each truffle in paper candy cup and chill for at least 1 hour before serving. Truffles can be stored in refrigerator about 1 week.

White or Chocolate Flavored Candy Coating

Combine ¼ lb. candy coating and 2 tablespoons shortening in a small double boiler or microwave until mixture melts. Using fork, dip each rolled truffle ball in candy coating. Place on prepared baking sheet. chill until set. Reheat chocolate candy and redip truffles and chill until coating is set.

Flavor Variation: Follow recipe above, except omit vanilla and substitute a flavored extract or liqueur (maple, almond, cherry, orange, peppermint, etc.)

Yield: 18 truffles.

Snow Eggs with Kahlúa, Chocolate and Custard Sauce

A delicious dessert that you will love to make.

3	large eggs, whites only
¼	cup granulated sugar
3	cups milk
2	tablespoons granulated sugar
½	tablespoon vegetable oil
1	Custard Sauce, *see page 216*
1	Kahlúa Chocolate Sauce, *see page 217*

Using an electric mixer, beat egg whites until soft peaks form. While still beating, add ¼ cup sugar, and beat until very firm.

In a small saucepan, heat milk and 2 tablespoons sugar to about 194° F. Bring to a very gentle simmer.

With a large kitchen spoon, form the beaten whites into 2 large egg shapes, smoothing their surfaces carefully with a metal spatula coated with oil. Gently lower each into the simmering *(not boiling)* milk, rinsing the spoon in cold water between each operation.

Poach shapes for 3 minutes on one side, turn and poach 3 minutes on the other side. With a slotted spoon, transfer the snow eggs to drain on a dish towel. They should be just firm to the touch, but still light and delicate.

Cover plates with a layer of custard sauce, and place one snow egg on each plate. Next, place chocolate sauce in a squeeze bottle, or using a small ladle, dribble designs on top of custard. Do not cover snow eggs. Serve immediately.

Yield: 2 servings

White-Laced Pecan Cookies with Fresh Berries

Thin crispy cookies that are shaped and filled with plain or flavored whipped cream.

4	Pecan-Laced Cookies, *see below*
¼	pint raspberries, washed
¼	pint blackberries, washed
¼	pint sliced strawberries
2	cups Romance Whipped Cream, *see page 217*
½	cup raspberry purée, *see page 216*

Prepare pecan-laced cookies, as shown *below*. Prepare a double batch of romance whipped cream using recipe *on page 217*, and store in refrigerator.

Place romance whipped cream in pastry bag and pipe out a large strip of whipped cream on each plate. Place two pecan-laced cookies on each plate, so they stand up, next pipe whipped cream on each side and inside cookies. Place berries inside cookies and a few outside. Dribble raspberry purée over top of berries. Serve immediately.

Yield: 2 to 3 servings

Pecan-Laced Cookies

Thin crispy cookie that is shaped and filled with plain or flavored whipped cream.

2	tablespoons butter or margarine
2	tablespoons firmly-packed brown sugar
2	tablespoons light corn syrup
3	tablespoons all-purpose flour
2	tablespoons pecans, chopped fine
½	teaspoon vanilla extract

Preheat oven to 350°F. Grease large baking sheet, and dust with flour

Melt butter in a small saucepan over low heat. Stir in brown sugar and corn syrup. Increase heat to high and bring mixture to a boil, stirring constantly until brown sugar dissolves.

Remove pan from heat. Stir in flour and pecans until well combined. Blend in vanilla. Let sit for 3 to 4 minutes.

Drop four equal parts of batter onto prepared baking sheets by using a rounded tablespoon, placed about 5 inches apart. With small spatula, spread batter on top of cookies. Bake until cookies are browned, about 8 to 10 minutes. Let stand on baking sheets until cookies are just firm enough to handle (30 seconds to 1 minute). Remove warm cookies from baking sheet one at a time with a spatula, and immediately drape over a rolling pin. Drape cookies with nutty sides up. When cool, transfer to a wire rack. If cookies become too cool to shape, return to oven for a few seconds until they are pliable again.

Yield: 4 cookies

Crepe Shells

Crepes, as you may know, are delicate, tissue-like pancakes.

¼	cup all-purpose flour
7	tablespoons milk
1	large egg
½	tablespoon vegetable oil
1	pinch of salt
1	vegetable spray or oil

Preparing Crepe Shells: In a blender or food processor, add flour, milk, egg, oil, and salt. Blend or process until it's a smooth batter, stopping a few times to scrape down the sides. Cover and refrigerate for 1 hour.

Blend batter well before making crepes. Over moderate heat, lightly oil a preheated 6–inch nonstick sauté pan. Add just enough batter for a thin coat. Tilt so batter forms a thin, even covering over the bottom of the pan. Cook each crepe until it sets, about 60 seconds. Turn and cook the other side for 45 seconds. Place cooked crepe on waxed paper or a clean, dry surface. Do not stack crepes while hot!

Cooled crepes may be stacked, or wrapped in aluminum foil, and refrigerated for a few days. They may also be frozen for up to a few months. Thaw in refrigerator for 6 hours before use.

Yield: 4 crepes

Glossary

Antipasto A first course of assorted relishes and seafood.

Bake To cook covered or uncovered in an oven or oven type appliance.

Beat To make mixture smooth by adding air with brisk whipping or stirring motion using spoon or electric mixer.

Béchamel Rich, white cream sauce.

Blanch To precook in boiling water or steam.

Blend To thoroughly mix two ingredients.

Boil To cook in liquid at boiling temperature (212°F.) where bubbles rise to the top.

Breaded To coat with bread crumbs before cooking.

Chill To place in refrigerator to reduce temperature.

Chop To cut in pieces about the size of peas.

Coulis A sauce made from ingredients that have been pureed and strained.

Crouton A small cube dry toasted bread served atop soup or salad.

Cut In To mix shortening with dry ingredients using pastry blender or knives or processor.

Dice To cut food in small cubes of uniform size and shape.

Dissolve To dissolve a dry substance in a liquid to form a solution.

Dredge To sprinkle or coat with flour or other fine substance.

Egg wash Whole egg, egg white, or yolk mixed with a small amount of water or milk.

Fillet A strip of fish without bone.

Flake To break lightly in small pieces.

Fold To add ingredients gently to a mixture. Using a spatula turn bowl for even distribution.

Francaise Coated with egg, Parmesan and chopped parsley then sauteed. Served with a lemon butter sauce.

French Knife Knife for chopping with a heavy 8-inch blade tapered to a slight point. Also known as a a chef's knife.

Fry To cook in hot shortening. Pan fry is to cook in small amount Deep fry is to cook immersed in large amount of grease or shortening.

Garnish	To trim with small pieces of colorful food.
Glaze	Mixture applied to food which hardens or becomes firm and or adds a glossy appearance.
Julienne	Match like strips of vegetables or fruits.
Marinate	To allow a food to stand in a liquid to tenderize or to add flavor.
Minced	To chop food in very small pieces.
Mirepoix	A mixture of roughly cut or diced vegetables, spices, and herbs used for flavoring.
Mix	To combine ingredients, usually by stirring, until evenly distributed.
Parboil	To cook partially in a boiling or simmering liquid.
Mornay	A cheese flavored white sauce.
Poach	To cook in hot liquid, being careful that food holds its shape while cooking.
Precook	To cook food partially or completely before final cooking or reheating.
Puree	A paste or thick liquid of food
Reduce	To cook by simmering or boiling until a certain quantity of liquid is decreases; usually done to concentrate flavors.
Roux	A mixture of flour and fat that is cooked and is used to thick en soups and sauces.
Sauté	To brown or cook in a small amount of hot shortening or oil.
Simmer	To cook in liquid over low heat at temperature of 185°F. to 210°F.
Stir	To mix ingredients with a circular motion until well blended.
Whip	To beat rapidly to incorporate air in and produce expansion, as in heavy cream or egg whites.

A

B

C

If you enjoyed this book, here are some other titles you might enjoy as well. To Request a complete catalog or to place an order, write to:

Lonnie T. Lynch
9850 Sandalfoot Blvd.
P.O. Box 226
Boca Raton Florida 33428-6645
Or visit our website at
www.romancecooking.com.

— Mastering the Art of —
CARVING WATERMELON CENTERPIECES

An entertaining 110 pages on how to carve watermelon centerpieces. With the easy-to-follow instructions and templates, anyone can prepare party centerpieces. From fish to Christmas tree and birds, there is a carving for every occasion. A perfect gift for someone who entertains a lot. Or, for the woman who has everything
Suggested Retail Price $9.95 ISBN 0-9628912-1-5
• 112 PAGES • SOFT COVER •

— Mastering the Art of —
CARVING MELON CENTERPIECES

Another entertaining 110 pages on how to carve melon centerpieces. Again with the easy-to-follow hand instructions and templates, anyone can carve melon party centerpieces. Over 30 melon designs with illustrated instructions of how to carve honeydew and cantaloupe centerpieces. From fourth of July carvings to I Love You and holidays, there is a carving for every occasion.
Suggested Retail Price $9.95 ISBN 0-9629277-1-6
• 112 PAGES • SOFT COVER •

— The Art of —

ROMANCE COOKING

Experience an Evening Romancing Your Relationship

The Art of Romance Cooking is about creating those special moments in which to appreciate each others companionship.

From candles, music, and food, Lonnie will inspire you to create and cook a romantic meal for you to enjoy together. Lonnie has been fortunate to have worked in beautiful and luxurious atmospheres to see the value that can be created for romancing your relationship.

Suggested Retail Price $14.95 ISBN 0-9629277-3-2

• 240 PAGES • SOFT COVER •

Featuring:

The Art of Romantic Feeding for Two Where You Will Experience a Breathtaking Evening Romancing Your Relationship.

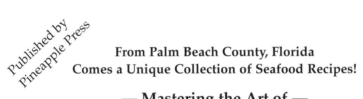

Published by Pineapple Press

**From Palm Beach County, Florida
Comes a Unique Collection of Seafood Recipes!**

— Mastering the Art of —

FLORIDA SEAFOOD

Lonnie is now ready to teach you the secrets he learned while preparing seafood in such fine eating establishments as the Boca Raton Hotel & Resort, Pete's Boca Raton, Firehouse Rest., Santa Fe Grille, Nick's Italian Fishery and country clubs, such as Aberdeen and Bocaire. From Stoned Crabs to Pompano, from Orange Pecan Barbecue Sauce to Old Floridian Grill Seasonings, Lonnie will teach you the art of creating beautiful and appealing seafood dishes.

Suggested Retail Price $12.95 ISBN 1-56164-176-6

• 170 PAGES • SOFT COVER •

Lonnie T. Lynch

9850 Sandalfoot Blvd.,
P.O. Box #226
Boca Raton, Florida 33428-6645
561-483-3751/Fax 561-558-0546
1-800-404-3569

Order Forms are Available
on the Web Site
http://www.romancecooking.com

Order Form

Ship to:
Name _____

C/O _____

Address _____

City _____ State _____

Zip _____

(Gift) Ship to: Item_____

Name _____

C/O _____

Address _____

City _____ State _____

Zip _____

(Gift) Ship to: Item_____

Name _____

C/O _____

Address _____

City _____ State _____

Zip _____

Please include your phone number. we'll call only if we have a question about your order.

Daytime phone ( ) _____ Evening phone ( ) _____

$3.00 Shipping Plus $.95 Handling Per Item • 1 book $3.95 • 2 books $4.90

Item	Product Description	Quantity	Price Each	Total

Method of Payment
❑ Check or Money Order
❑ Credit Card Circle One

VISA   MASTERCARD

Card # _____

Exp Date _____

Signature#_____

SUBTOTAL [   ]

Book Subtotal [   ]

FL Sales Tax [   ]

Total S&H [   ]
See S&H cart to calculate

Total [   ]

Delivery - Method Ship

Time	Total Shipping Price (add both columns) Per Order	Per Item
Standard Ground • 3 to 6 business days	$3.00 per order plus	$0.95 S/H

Terms of Use, Copyright, and Privacy Policy Copyright 2000 Lonnie T. Lynch

Return Policy Satisfaction Guaranteed Books returned within 30 days of receipt have a full refund privilege. If you have any question or problems, call our customer service at 1-800-404-3569 or send to Lonnie T. Lynch